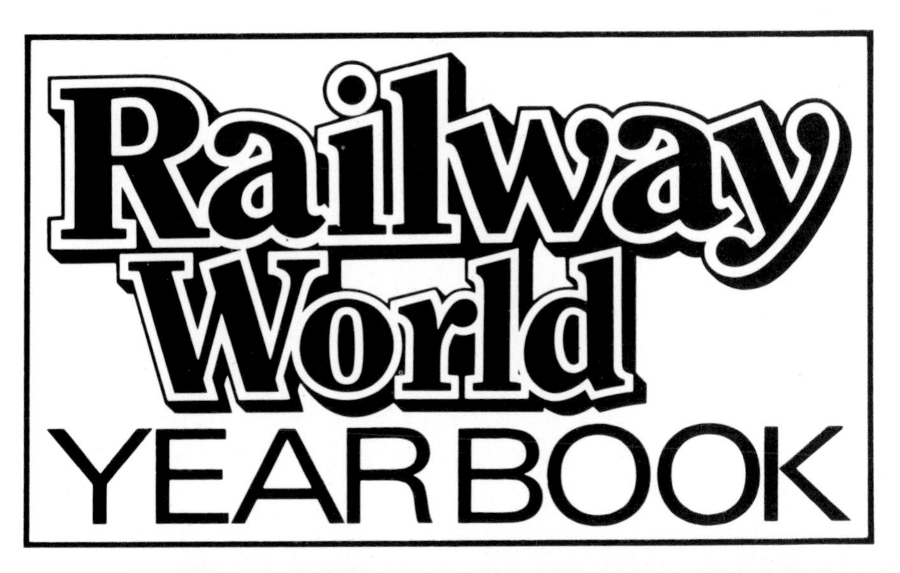

Front cover:
Norton Junction is the location as 'Hall' No 6908 *Downham Hall*, minus its nameplates, passes with a freight working in 1965. *M. Mensing*

Back cover:
Preserved Great Northern Railway (Ireland) compound 4-4-0 No 85 leaves Belfast past Adelaide station with the stock from the 'Shannon Railtour', en route from Belfast Central to Portrush and Whitehead on 16 May 1988. *Nick Bartlett*

Below:
The Severn Valley Railway's Ivatt Class 4 2-6-0 No 43106 shows a clean face to the world at Bridgnorth shed on 31 July 1988. *Colin Boocock*

Only the shortest piece of the Westoe colliery electric coal railway at South Shields remains today, so quickly do things change from one year to the next! Today, diesels work most of the system and electric working only covers the stretch from the Battery Sidings to Harton Low Staithes, where electric locomotive No 15 is seen propelling another load of coal to the unloading shed. *Colin Boocock*

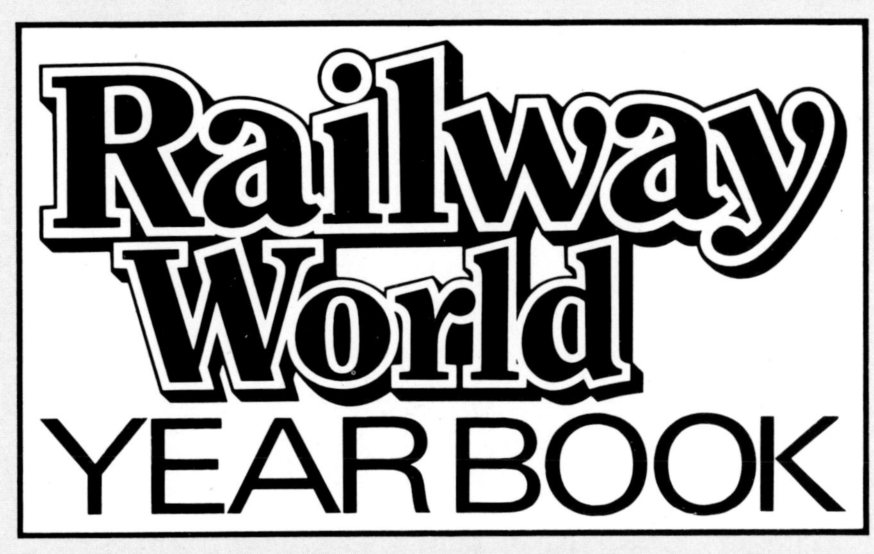

Edited by Colin Boocock

LONDON
IAN ALLAN LTD

Contents

Railtalk *Colin Boocock* 5

The Railway Queen *Dulcie M. Ashdown* 6

Photo Feature: Steam in the West Midlands *Colin Boocock* 9

Accidents always come in threes *Stanley Hall* 12

Miracles at Colwich *Colin Boocock* 17

To Kemmannugundi on the Narrow Gauge *Allan C. Baker* 21

Photo feature: Severn Valley variety *Hugh Ballantyne* 28

The rebuilt 'Merchant Navy' class: Britain's finest Pacifics? *Colin Boocock* 30

Photo Feature: Modern Freight on BR 36

The G&Q steams on: Update on the railways of Ecuador *Gil Hughes* 38

At the Time of Going to Press: British Steam Locomotive Update *Michael Harris* 43

High Speed Train through the Severn Tunnel *Robin Russell* 49

Mixed feelings: A Journey on the Sligo, Leitrim & Northern Counties Railway *Robin Stieber* 55

Photo Feature: There are still Trams at Blackpool! *Colin Boocock* 60

Scottish Stations 1923-1988 *J. L. Stevenson* 63

Photo Feature: Shadows of Industrial Steam 68

Grandfather's Railway *Colin Boocock* 71

Quiz: Spot the difference 76

Photo-quiz 76

Wordsearch 78

Answers to quiz 79

First published 1989

ISBN 0 7110 1865 0

Published by Ian Allan Ltd, Shepperton, Surrey; and printed by Ian Allan Printing Ltd at their works at Coombelands in Runnymede, England

Railtalk

Colin Boocock

Looking back over the 1989 *Railway World Year Book* one cannot fail to be surprised at how quickly changes come to the railways we like so much.

At about the time that the 1989 Year Book went to press, British Rail announced that the 1987/88 financial year was its best ever, following an unprecedented upsurge in traffic. Electric services were inaugurated to Weymouth and between Watford and St Albans. The Thameslink cross-London service opened new north-south travel opportunities. The first electric locomotives of Classes 90 and 91 began their development trials, and most will be in full service by the time this new Year Book appears. The first driving van trailers have since appeared, to initiate push-pull working on the West Coast main line expresses.

Many steam locomotives have entered or re-entered service on preserved railways in this country. Elsewhere in this issue Michael Harris brings us up to date with progress in the preservation field.

A few favourites have disappeared from our railways. BR's Class 45s have gone, apart from the one green special survivor. Sprinter diesel multiple-units have appeared on trains in the southwest and the north, and in Scotland, taking away from several lines the thrill of riding the hills behind diesel favourites like the 31/4s, 33s, 37/4s and 47/4s. British Coal's railway which linked Westoe colliery in South Shields with Harton Low Staithes on the Tyne (see the 1989 *Year Book*) has virtually lost its electric traction, which last year we thought had many years left in it.

The three disparate train crashes in the 1988/89 winter at Clapham, Purley and Bellgrove (Glasgow) leave us all in mourning. We pray nonetheless that high rail safety will continue to be the norm.

Amid all this change and activity remain our memories. This Year Book for 1990 unashamedly brings back the past, for the nostalgia of those who were there and for the interest of those who were not. The book blends the present day with history; and home railways with overseas. We are certain there will be something in it for you!

Colin Boocock

Acknowledgements

A touch of humour is always welcome. I could not resist including some more of Alan Thorpe's cartoons. They have all appeared from time to time in the magazine of the Bournemouth Railway Club, *BRC News*, to whose editor, Tony Jervis, I offer grateful thanks for permission to reproduce them here.

The article on the Severn Tunnel has an unusual twist. The experience of travelling on an InterCity 125 set through the tunnel is related from the eyes of a visitor to Great Britain from New Zealand, Robin Russell.

To others who have responded to my requests for material I am grateful. Timescales are often tight and, as before, I have ended up with more material than I can use.

CPB

Below:
Sprinters' working diagrams now take these successful diesel units as far afield as Cornwall and Scotland. No 155304 was stabled at Penzance when photographed on 16 September 1988. *Colin Boocock*

The Railway Queen

Dulcie M. Ashdown

'We went to see the railroad near Hersham [in Surrey],' wrote 17-year-old Princess Victoria in her journal on 8 February 1837, 'and saw the steam carriage pass with surprising quickness, striking sparks as it flew along the railroad, enveloped in clouds of smoke and making a loud noise. It is a curious thing indeed!'

Four months later, Victoria became queen.

In 1837 Britain had about 1,000 miles of 'railroad'. When Victoria opened the Great Exhibition in 1851, the mileage had increased almost sevenfold; 20 years later, it had nearly doubled again, and by the end of the Queen's long life — she died in 1901 — she had travelled many thousands of miles by train, in Britain and abroad.

The Great Western Railway (GWR) won the accolade of providing the young Queen with her first train ride: in June 1842 she travelled to London from Slough (then the nearest station to Windsor) — 'Not so fast next time, Mr Conductor,' Victoria's Albert is said to have remarked, having completed the journey in the then breathtaking time of 25min.

The Prince was fascinated by what we now call technology, the Queen by novel sensations — the impression of speed, the smoothness of running on rails after the jolting of horse-drawn carriages, and the sight of town and country flying past.

However, when the royal family travelled on the same line in the summer of 1842, returning from a holiday in Kent, the journey was not so amusing. Somehow they had been separated from the children's nursemaids, and the Queen and her ladies were left to cope alone with Vicky, aged two, and Bertie, aged one. According to one of the party, the royal children were 'taken with tearing spirits and a rage for climbing, crawling, poking into corners [of the railway carriage] and — after a little time — being tired, cross and squally for hours'.

Until 1849 the Queen had to transfer to a horsedrawn carriage at Slough to complete the journey to Windsor, but in that year the London & South Western Railway (LSWR) completed its line to Windsor and Eton Riverside station, a mile from the castle. Then, just two months later, the GWR brought its own track into the town itself, planting a station in the morning shadow of the castle walls. That did not, however, mean that the Queen immediately discarded Riverside, for the LSWR still offered the only through service from London: leaving from Paddington, Victoria still had to change at Slough, for the GWR had short-sightedly laid standard gauge instead of a 7ft gauge track on the branch line to Windsor. The error was remedied in 1862, and thereafter the town station saw a flow of royal passengers, foreign cousins and government dignitaries, and the Queen's messengers who daily brought state papers from Whitehall.

Today the grandiose station is used mainly by tourists, but it has a permanent royal presence in the Tussaud waxworks of Queen Victoria and members of her family which form part of the 'Royalty and Railways' exhibition there.

Within a decade of her first train ride, Queen victoria was an experienced rail traveller. She and Albert and their nine children would not only use the town station whenever their presence was required in London but leave from the Riverside station for Gosport in Hampshire, there to take ship for their holiday home, Osborne House on the Isle of Wight. Gosport had a special branch line into the Royal Navy Dockyard (and a temple-like station there) to take the family direct to the Royal Yacht.

Other holidays were spent at Balmoral Castle, on Deeside in Scotland, whose nearest station was Ballater (now disused). Scots Sabbatarians were scandalised that the line was kept open on Sundays, when all others were closed, so that despatches could come swiftly from London. The Queen, not so strict herself, had to give way to public opinion when, needing to travel on a Sunday, she found herself having to get up at crack of dawn in order to reach Aberdeen in time for morning service there before continuing her journey.

On her first through journey to Ballater in 1850, Victoria made two stops to open new bridges over the Tyne and the Tweed. She loved the view from high lines and bridges — her engine driver was always under instruction to slow down when her train went over Wharncliffe Viaduct at Hanwell on the GWR's line to Slough and Windsor, so that Her Majesty might enjoy the panorama over what was then a rural landscape.

But the Queen must have shuddered when, in December 1879, she heard of a train plunging off the great Tay Bridge in Scotland, drowning about a hundred people in the river's icy water. Prime Minister Disraeli wrote to her that the event had 'rather shaken' his nerves, occurring as it did only six months after she had crossed the bridge herself — 'He entreats Your Majesty to deign to be cautious,' he wrote to Victoria in the formal third-person style.

She had no need of warning. There had been so many accidents on the railways in the half-century of their existence that she remarked that directors of the various companies ought to travel on each and every train — 'We should soon see a different state of things!'.

Over the years the companies vied with each other to provide the royal family with all the comforts of home when they went on their travels. The Great Northern set a high standard of luxury when, in 1851, each of the three carriages for the royal family and their attendants boasted a 'withdrawing-room' with the latest thing in sanitary fitments, and each window opened at the touch of a finger, with an ingenious counterbalance device.

But no royal carriage was more sumptuous than that now on show in York, at the National Railway Museum. Built by the London & North Western Railway (LNWR), it has padded velvet chairs and sofas — and padded ceilings to match, rich gilding and numerous bell-pushes that could be used to summon servants, or even to stop the train!

That the Queen made good use of the bells was witnessed by one of her granddaughters, Princess Victoria ('Moretta') of Prussia, when in 1889 she accompanied her 70-year-old grandmother on an overnight journey to Balmoral. The Princess wrote home that her grandmother had taken hours to settle in their shared sleeping car, summoning her maid time and again to bring or take away a shawl, open or close a window, and make a hot drink.

By then, Queen Victoria had made many rail journeys abroad, some to visit relations and heads of state, more for her own pleasure — in the last decades of her life she made a spring trip almost annually to a sunny foreign resort, generally on the French Riviera.

Transporting Queen Victoria from the port of Cherbourg, where she left the royal yacht after the channel crossing, to her destination in the south, must have been an annual nightmare for officials of the French railway system. It was not a matter of delivering one old lady and her luggage: apart from any members of the royal family who travelled with the Queen, there were ladies-in-waiting and equerries, maids and footmen, cooks and

Left:
Queen Victoria encouraged many great engineering feats in her era. This view shows her taking a regal interest in the first Tay bridge in 1879.
Illustrated London News Picture Library

Above right:
To take commercial advantage of royalty was not unheard of in the last century. This Cadbury's cocoa advertisement of 1884 perports to show the Queen in the royal train, presumably drinking cocoa. The outline of Windsor castle can be seen through the opposite carriage window. *Illustrated London News Picture Library*

Below:
There were several developments of the Royal Train on the London & North Western Railway. This is the 1887 train (headed by Webb compound 2-2-2-0 No 410 *City of Liverpool*). The Queen's carriage is the twin unit on 6-wheeled underframes forming the sixth vehicle behind the tender.
Courtesy of the National Railway Museum, York

Above:
In 1894 Queen Victoria rode in this magnificent LNWR 12-wheeler. This coach is now part of the National Collection. *Courtesy of the National Railway Museum, York*

Bottom right:
The Great Western station at Windsor was used frequently by Her Majesty. The station's long association with royalty is now recorded in a permanent exhibition there. This view shows the station entrance in 1985. *Colin Boocock*

grooms — the latter to tend the horses which travelled with the Queen, and her donkey, and their respective carriage and cart, plus a vast amount of household equipment from the Queen's own bed down to the cooks' favourite utensils. And this was even required when the Queen was staying in a hotel, for she would take over one or two whole floors and be independent of the hotel's catering and services. On the continent Queen Victoria travelled in railway coaches made, and between holidays stored, in Belgium.

Belgium! It was a Belgian rail journey that nearly robbed Victoria of her heir, her eldest son, Bertie. One day in the year 1900, as their train pulled out of the railway station at Brussels, a teenaged anarchist fired directly at the Prince of Wales, sending several bullets into his compartment, one of which lodged in the seat beside him. In Britain, there had been seven attempts on Queen Victoria's life over the years, mainly while she was riding in horsedrawn carriages. In Russia, back in 1888, when an imperial train carrying Tsar Alexander III and his family had become derailed, no one knew if it was an accident or the work of anarchists. The giant Tsar held up the roof of the carriage to allow his wife and children to escape, and managed to join them.

Perhaps it was fear of an accident on foreign soil that limited the speed of Queen Victoria's French trains to 35mph during the day and 25mph at night. If that was not enough to wreak havoc with the national schedules, she insisted on frequent stops along the route. The first was for an hour in the morning, to enable the Queen and her ladies to dress (though the men of the party must have blessed her even more, being able to shave without cutting their throats); then there must be stops for each meal, which would be ordered in advance and brought aboard at a convenient station. The Queen always carried with her flasks of Irish stew made at Windsor, wrapped in red flannel 'cushions' to keep them warm, but she was rarely known to ask for stew when there was some foreign delicacy as an alternative. Another commodity put aboard frequently was ice — not for drinks but to be piled in footbaths and placed in the drawing room car to cool it, for Victoria felt the heat intensely.

The loading and unloading, the timing of the Royal Train not to interfere too much with main-line schedules, the delivery of food (hot) at the right moment, the placing of undercover detectives to sniff out anarchists' plots — how many French railways officials and stationmasters must have cursed the little woman who called herself 'The Countess of Kent' on her travels, even though everyone knew her real identity.

In the middle of this maelstrom the Queen would sit serenely, interested in everything that happened, always ready to be 'amused', by no means the doleful and censorious figure of 20th-century caricature but laughing heartily if not frequently, appreciative of good food, music, fine countryside and the thrill of foreign travel.

A lady-in-waiting once remarked that royal children must think that 'the populace' existed only to cheer and wave whenever a royal train halted in their town. Queen Victoria knew her people better. Through the railways she travelled more widely than any of her ancestors since the crusader kings of the Middle Ages, and whereas carriage routes would detour away from slums and industry, trains gave her glimpses of real life from which she might draw her own conclusions as to the state of the nation. At the same time, the Queen was seen by vast numbers of her subjects, in every corner of her kingdom, because she could travel so easily to visit them — as they, on their excursion trains, could travel to 'look at the Queen'.

Victoria died in January 1901, at Osborne House on the Isle of Wight. Her coffin was put on a train at the Royal Naval Dockyard at Gosport and then travelled the familiar line to Victoria station in London, thence from Paddingnton to Windsor, for burial. As the trains passed by, all along the track people knelt down, in fields and on roadsides, watching the last journey of the Queen whose reign had seen the social revolution brought about by the railways.

Photo Feature:

Steam in the West Midlands

Colin Boocock

In July 1955 a young railway photographer visited the principal stations in the West Midlands with his father's old folding Nagel camera. The photographs which follow are the result of those enjoyable three days.

Above:
Lined black 'County' class 4-6-0 No 1003 *County of Wilts* at the head of a Birkenhead to Paddington express on 15 July 1955, brings a motley collection of ex-GWR coaches into Wolverhampton Low Level station's up platform. The stock is all in BR carmine red and cream livery. *Colin Boocock*

Below:
Class 5 4-6-0s were part of the staple traction diet at Birmingham New Street. On 14 July 1955 No 44870 enters the station from the east end. *Colin Boocock*

Above:
The 'Cambrian Coast Express' was still formed entirely of ex-GWR corridor coaches of various styles in 1955. The up train approaches Snow Hill behind 'Castle' class 4-6-0 No 5040 *Stokesay Castle*. Note the distinctive high-mounted signal cabin on the left. *Colin Boocock*

Top left:
Snow Hill station was approached by a long dark tunnel, out of which emerges Churchward class 28XX 2-8-0 No 2871 with a heavy coal train. *Colin Boocock*

Top:
The GWR had two diesel parcels cars, one with 'streamlined' outline and one with the later, more angular form. On 14 July 1955 No W17W, the streamlined one, passes rapidly through Birmingham Snow Hill heading towards Wolverhampton.
Colin Boocock

Left:
No 5955 *Garth Hall* was in BR black livery lined in red, cream and grey when photographed at Snow Hill's main up platform with a Portsmouth train on the same day. The carriages are a mixture of former GWR, SR and new BR. *Colin Boocock*

Right:
Former LNWR 0-8-0 No 49146 trundles under a classic GWR signal gantry at the north end of Shrewsbury station on 15 July 1955. *Colin Boocock*

Left:
Not long after it had been transferred to the London Midland Region following its four-year spell on the Southern, 1 Co-Co 1 1,750hp diesel-electric No 10201 attracts an inquisitive audience as it prepares to leave Birmingham New Street with a Euston express service on 13 July 1955. *Colin Boocock*

Below:
The joint nature of railway operations around Shrewsbury is emphasised by this view of WR 'County' 4-6-0 No 1025 *County of Radnor* standing alongside LMR Fowler 2-6-4T No 42390 at the south end of the station. *Colin Boocock*

Accidents always come in threes

Stanley Hall

Conington is a sleepy little village just off the Great North Road, and has no great claim to fame apart perhaps from its archaeological remains. The East Coast main line passes about a mile to the east but there was never a Conington station. There was, however, a signalbox, which the railway company, in the cavalier manner of 19th-century railway companies, insisted on spelling as Connington. Until World War 2 it was merely a block post with an engineer's tip, but increased wartime traffic caused some new sidings to be built there to ease the pressure on the giant New England marshalling yards 10 miles further north at Peterborough, and an extra signalbox was built, the two boxes then becoming known as Connington North and Connington South. The sidings ceased to be used in the 1960s but the signalboxes survived until 1975, when they were swept away by the Peterborough resignalling scheme.

To the passenger in one of today's East Coast main line expresses, Connington is nothing more than a passing glimpse of rows of Engineer's wagons on a tip in the middle of nowhere, but in the 1960s Connington was witness to a remarkable series of accidents. The first one occurred on the night of Friday 15 December 1961, when frost and fog were widespread. There were four tracks then between Connington South and Huntingdon, with the main lines in the centre and goods lines on the outside. The up goods line from Connington South to Abbots Ripton, four miles to the south and the scene of a famous double collision on 21 January 1876, was worked under the Permissive Block system, under which goods trains were allowed to follow each other neck and neck, essential in those days to cope with the heavy flow of goods trains. An unfitted (ie unbraked) goods train had been sent up the goods line, and was followed 11min later by a fully-fitted express goods, the 9.50pm Class C New England to King's Cross Goods, hauled by a 'V2' 2-6-2 No 60803 (34E). Some 8min later 'Deltic' No D9012 (34G) on a train of empty stock, the 9.55am Class C Newcastle to Holloway, joined the slowly-moving queue. This rather archaic method of working goods traffic was a relic of earlier days when goods trains habitually ran much more slowly, and it really ought to have had no place in the railways of the 1960s, but with the old-fashioned equipment then in use it was the only way the traffic could be handled, even though it was less than 100% safe, especially during fog. The driver of No 60803, peering into the fog for the tail light of the train in front, was proceeding very gently, quite unaware that he was being rapidly overtaken by the 'Deltic'-hauled train, which was travelling about 20mph faster. Its driver was also peering into the fog but he saw nothing until the outline

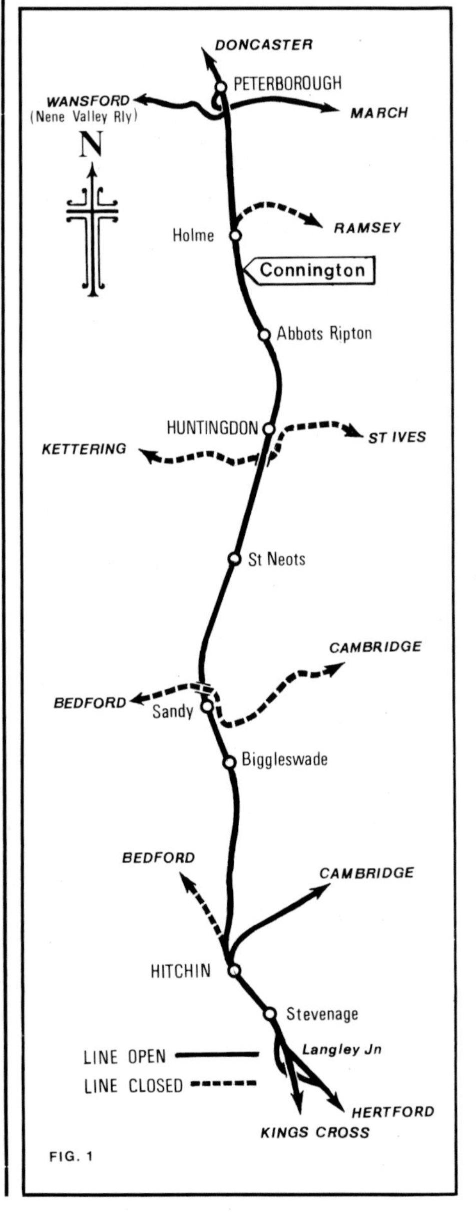

Below:
The fourth train to become entangled in the Connington crash of 15 December 1961 was the 10.05am Aberdeen-King's Cross meat train, headed by 'V2' 2-6-2 No 60977. This is how the *Hunts Post* of 21 December 1961 recorded its fate. *Huntingdon Post*

SMASH IN FOG

of the brakevan of the train in front suddenly appeared only a few yards away. A collision was inevitable.

The impact, at a closing speed of about 20mph, threw the brakevan across both main lines and a situation of potentially disastrous dimensions suddenly arose. Supposing a train, or, worse still, two trains, were approaching under clear signals on the main lines. Could they be saved from running into the wreckage themelves? The signalmen at Connington South and Abbots Ripton knew nothing about the accident; only the train crews of the crashed trains could save the day, and then only if they had time to act effectively, by running towards the approaching trains waving red lights and putting down detonators (exploding fog-signals) as a warning to the drivers that the line was blocked and that they must stop their trains as quickly as possible. Such a procedure obviously takes time and as luck had it there was little or none available that night.

The first crash occurred at about 10.15pm, just as another express goods, the 8.10pm Class C King's Cross to Newcastle, hauled by 'A3' Pacific No 60078 *Night Hawk* (52A) was rushing through Abbots Ripton on the main line at 50mph. Its unfortunate driver had no warning at all of imminent disaster and he ploughed into the derailed brakevan at full speed. His engine turned over on to its side, whilst the wagons of his train were hurled in all directions like toys. All lines were now completely blocked. But fate had not yet played its full hand.

At the very moment of the second collision another 'V2', No 60977 (50A), was approaching Connington on the up main line at full speed on the 10.05am meat train from Aberdeen to King's Cross. The Aberdeen fish and meat trains were always regarded as being well up the league table of crack freight trains and they certainly did not hang about. Signalmen took good care not to delay them and all the signals at Connington were green. Although Connington South signalbox was little more than a mile away from the scene of the accident the signalman had no idea that anything was wrong. He watched the Aberdeen meat hurry past his box, with its wagon wheels beating a clattering tattoo on his points and crossings, and he saw its tail light disappear into the fog.

The only thing that could possibly save it now was some emergency action on the part of the traincrews of the crashed trains, assuming that they were uninjured and capable of responding quickly. The first collision occured at 10.15pm and the rules said that the guard of the 'Deltic'-hauled train was responsible for giving the alarm if the up main *was* blocked. He was travelling at the front of his train and when he got out after the crash and walked to the engine he saw that the Up Main was blocked. He then set off back to warn any train approaching on that line, but was overtaken by the secondman of the 'Deltic', who managed to get about six coach-lengths beyond the end of his train when he heard the Aberdeen Meat approaching. He quickly put detonators on the line then leapt clear, just as the 'V2' thundered past. Its driver heard the detonators explode and immediately threw on all his brakes, but he was still travelling at about 30mph when he ploughed into the pile of wreckage. Eight minutes had elapsed between the first and last collisions, barely time for more distant warning to have been given, although it could have been done if the train crews had acted instantly and rushed back to safeguard the line, thus enabling the Aberdeen Meat to be stopped clear of the wreckage, or at least to be slowed down to well below 30mph.

However, the real culprit was the method of working trains on the goods line, allowing them to follow one another neck and neck like trams even during fog, with only one flickering oil lamp to warn the driver of a second train about the position of the one in front. It was a system which dated back to the early days of railways and may have been acceptable when goods trains habitually ran slowly and when brakevans always carried three lamps, but by 1961 fully-fitted goods trains only carried one, because often there were wagons behind the brakevan to facilitate attaching and detaching at intermediate yards, and wagons did not have brackets for the extra lamps. Incidentally, some years later the rules were changed to prohibit a second train from following a fully-fitted train under the neck and neck arrangements during fog, but that was brought about by the removal of brakevans from fully-fitted goods trains.

There had been what many people regarded as a retrograde change in the rules shortly before the accident. Up to October 1960 a signalman was required to show a green light to the

Fig 1
Location of Connington on the East Coast main line.

Below:
One of the endless stream of coal trains from New England to Ferme Park (London) enters Peterborough North in the charge of 'Austerity' 2-8-0 No 90665 of New England shed on 11 May 1953. Many of these trains went up the goods line from Connington South. *R. E. Vincent*

driver of a goods train following a train in front neck and neck, and this warned him positively that there was a train just in front. Indeed, the LMS and GWR had gone even further, and signalmen on those lines were required additionally to *tell* the driver about the state of the line ahead. On the LNER, however, such verbal warnings were only given in some of the Areas, and even then only where possible. On the Southern Area (ex GN) they were not required to be given at all, although it is interesting to recall that the signalmen at Connington South made a practice of indicating to drivers whether there was a train in front or not, by raising one finger and calling out 'One in'. It helped drivers of heavy goods trains faced with the 1 in 200 rising gradient, and was a sensible and practical, though unofficial, procedure.

However, the 1960 rule changes swept away nearly all those safeguards, and all that the signalman was required to do was to bring the tain nearly to a stand at the Home signal. This was supposed to be sufficient warning to a driver that there was a train somewhere in front! Still, old habits died hard at Connington. When No 60803, on the New England — King's Cross fitted, passed his box the signalman called out to the driver that there was a train in front. Unfortunately he did not do so when the 'Deltic'-hauled train passed his box a few minutes later. Such inconsistencies do not improve safey, and it is at least possible that the 'Deltic' driver was under the impression that the line was clear to the next signalbox. He would hardly have driven at 30mph in fog had he thought otherwise.

The actual regulations in force before the standardised change in October 1960, concerning the method of warning drivers that they were entering a section of permissive goods line on which there was already a train in front, were:

GWR	The train was stopped at the home signal, which was then cleared to allow the train to draw forward to the signalbox, where the driver was told how many trains were in front. He was also shown a green flag or light as a further warning to proceed cautiously.
LMSR	Very similar to GWR
LNER (NE Area)	The train was stopped at the home signal, which was then cleared after the driver had whistled an acknowledgement of a green flag or light shown by the signalman. *Where possible* the driver was told to proceed cautiously and how many trains were in front.
LNER (GN Sec)	Similar to NE Area, but no verbal warning.

The standardised Regulation introduced in October 1960 merely said:- 'The train must be brought nearly to a stand at the Home signal before it is cleared.'

No green flag, no warning, the reason being that at some places it was difficult for the driver to see the green flag or light, or that he did not pass close enough to the signalbox to receive a verbal message. the method of using the green flag or light was also thought to create the possibility of confusion with other regulations. It is difficult to accept such explanations, when one considers that the GWR and the LMS, and even the North Eastern area of the LNER, had managed safely with their own arrangements for many years, and they were all better than the new system, which threw almost all the responsibility for safety on to the driver. All these problems could have been avoided if money had been spent on the signalling system, because all that was required was the provision of a calling-on signal (a miniature arm placed underneath the main signal) so that drivers would know with certainty whether the line was clear to the next signalbox or whether there was a train in front. However, none were provided at Connington, which might be regarded as an unfortunate lapse on such an important main line, a lapse that would have proved really disastrous if the two trains on the main line that night had been express passenger trains instead of goods trains.

The use of a green flag to indicate caution may be thought strange, but this can be traced back to the 19th century, when green was always used in signals to indicate caution. White was used to indicate clear, until experience showed that extraneous white lights could be mistaken for a clear signal light by drivers, after which the signals were changed to the more familiar green for Clear. However, the use of green flags in signalboxes to indicate caution has lasted till the present day. Such use has also survived in hand signals given to drivers by shunters:-

Move away — White light waved slowly up and down.
Move away slowly — Green light waved slowly up and down.

The use of a single red light at the rear of a freight train came into operation on the LNER many years ago (it was certainly in use in the NE area when the LNER was formed in 1923) on those express goods trains which had the continuous automatic vacuum brake operational throughout the train, and were known as 'fully-fitted'. At one time *all* trains carried a red tail lamp and two red side lamps but eventually the requirement for passenger trains to carry side lamps was dropped, although goods trains continued to carry them. The side lights showed a red light towards the rear and a white light towards the front, so that the driver and fireman could check that their train was complete and had not broken in two. If a fully-fitted train splits in two (a rare occurrence) the brakes are automatically applied on both sections. Three red lights at the back of a train present an arresting image to a driver approaching from the rear, and on four-track sections, where drivers on the main line overtake trains on goods lines, one of the red side lights of a train on the goods lines is changed to white, to indicate that such a train really *is* on the goods line and not the main line, thus avoiding the driver on the main line wondering whether he ought to slam on his brakes. However, side lights are now almost a thing of the past, but it is evident that BR is not happy with a single red light at the rear of a train as all DMUs and EMUs now have two red tail lights and experiments are being conducted with a flashing red tail lamp. Railway history is full of such interesting little snippets.

In concluding this episode it is pleasing to be able to report that none of the traincrews involved was seriously injured, and that Calling-on signals were subsequently provided at Connington South.

The second Connington accident happened during the early hours of Tuesday 20 September 1966 by which time the continental clock had arrived and, as in the 1961

Above:
A resplendent 'A3' Pacific, No 60078 *Night Hawk* simmers gently at Darlington shed on 24 April 1955. This was one of the engines which came to grief at Connington on 15 December 1961. *K. R. Pirt*

Above right:
Part of the everyday scene in steam days, 'B1' class 4-6-0 No 61091 passes Abbots Ripton with a fully fitted express freight train.
The late Eric Treacy/P. B. Whitehouse Collection

accident, the weather was foggy. The driver of the 22.30 Sleeper from Edinburgh to King's Cross had been experiencing trouble with his 'Deltic' loco D9006 and he finally came to a stand at Connington South home signal. He reported the failure to the signalman, and it was decided to use a following freight train to push the express to Abbots Ripton, four miles away, where another loco was available to take it forward to King's Cross. The guard therefore set off to walk back to Connington North signalbox, about a mile away, in order to ride on the loco of the freight train and point out to its driver exactly where the express was standing, so that he did not come upon it unawares and crash into it. The guard also put detonators on the rails at 40 yards, 120 yards, and 200 yards from the rear of his train to help the driver of the assisting train in the darkness and fog.

The assisting train was the 22.15 from Tees Yard to Temple Mills, heavily loaded with steel, and hauled by a Type 4 Diesel-Electric No D168. It was fully-braked throughout. The guard climbed up into the driving cab and there was some discussion as to what was to be done but it is obvious from subsequent events that driver and guard had a different understanding as to where the detonators were placed. The train set off into the section and was soon going 'quite hard' according to the guard. However, he did not say anything to the driver about it. When the first detonator, only 200 yards from the express, was exploded the guard said 'That's the first one'. He knew the express was only 200 yards ahead in the fog but the driver assumed that it was at least ¼-mile away, although he braked the train slightly. Within a few seconds the next detonator was exploded and before anyone could do anthing the red tail light of the express suddenly appeared out of the fog. The driver slammed on his brakes but could not stop. He was too near and going too fast, and although he managed to reduce his speed to less than 10mph his train, weighing 865 tons, hit the standing express with a fearful wallop. All the coaches were damaged and several passengers had to be taken to hospital.

After the accident BR changed the Rules. The assisting train then had to be brought to a stand on exploding a detonator ¼-mile from the failed train, after which it had to proceed cautiously to another detonator 100 yards from the failed train. During fog the assisting train had to be stopped again, and the guard had to get down on to the track and proceed on foot, guiding the driver by hand signal. This certainly tightened up matters, but instances continue to occur to this day where assisting locos or trains crash into the very trains they are going to assist.

After two accidents railway pundits always say 'They come in threes'. Nor was there long to wait for what was in several ways the most serious accident of the three.

On Sunday 5 March 1967 the 22.30 express from King's Cross to Edinburgh (the sister of the train involved in the 1966 accident) left King's Cross on time with 11 coaches hauled by 'Deltic' D9004. It was marshalled: brakevan, three Post Office sorting vans, one sleeping car, five coaches, and brakevan and carried 147 passengers. The train ran easily, and was coasting down the falling gradient past Connington South at about 75mph when it suddenly became derailed beneath the seventh vehicle. The train split in two behind that vehicle and the front portion ran on for 600 yards before being brought to a stand by the automatic application of the vacuum brake, at the exact spot of the collision six months earlier. A quarter of a mile behind, the eighth and ninth vehicles lay on their sides. Five passengers died and 18 were injured.

When serious accidents like this occur, the railway authorities have a number of different priorities, after the security of the line has been achieved to prevent further trains from running into the wreckage. Naturally, the first one is to rescue the injured and have them taken off to hospital with the least possible delay. A second one is to clear away the wreckage and restore the track and signalling as soon as possible so that the line can be reopened. But it is also important to establish the cause of the accident before the evidence is disturbed or removed, so that any lessons can be learned and changes in equipment or procedures introduced. This detective work must start at once, but at Connington the investigators were baffled. They could find no explanation for the derailment, but they discovered marks on the facing points to the down goods line just past the signalbox, which seemed to indicate that the points had moved as the train was passing over them. Such a movement should have been impossible, because the points were physically bolted by a locking apparatus worked by a lever in the signalbox. That lever in turn was locked by the junction signal being cleared. As long as that signal was at clear the lever releasing the point lock was itself locked. If the signal had been put back to danger before the train passed it the driver would have seen it and stopped. As soon as the train passed the signal it occupied a track-circuit (an electrical train-detection device operated through the rails) which not only locked the lever working the points lock but also the lever working the points themselves. These arrangements are standard at most facing points and are designed to ensure that the points cannot be moved irregularly by the signalman, either by mistake or deliberately, although it seems inconceivable that a signalman would attempt such a dangerous act on purpose. However, it was discovered that at Connington South signalbox there was a distance of 58ft between the junction signal and the start of the track-circuit that locked the points, and that if the signalman put the junction signal back to danger at the instant it went out of the driver's sight as he passed under it there was a fraction of a second during which the signalman could release the lever of the points lock before it became relocked by the occupation of the track-circuit. With the points now unlocked they were free to be moved even as the train passed over them provided the electrical lock on the points lever itself had been freed in some way. And yet it seemed such a remote possibility. Surely, no signalman would do such a thing. The investigators pondered and repondered the evidence. They called in other experts. They held trials and carried out a whole series of tests and experiments. They questioned and requestioned the signalman, but he was adamant that he had not moved the points. And so the Connington South derailment looked set to join the Grantham high speed derailment of 1906, and the Marie Celeste, as the great unsolved mysteries of the 20th century.

And so it might have been. The months passed without a solution, and the investigators grew more and more disconsolate, wondering if they had missed a vital clue. It was crucial that they discovered the cause, in case there was some latent danger that could recur and cause another derailment. But as tests and investigations continued the evidence more and more pointed to the signalman's having carried out a series of irregular actions, and caused the derailment. Furthermore such actions could only have been done deliberately. There was no way that they could have been done mistakenly or unintentionally. What perhaps clinched matters was the discovery of marks on the lock controlling the points lever which seemed to indicate that the lock had been tampered with. Could the unthinkable be true? Could an experienced main-line signalman really have done such a thing? The answer to that question is almost certainly 'no', but the signalman was not experienced. He was 20-years-old and had been recruited 'straight off the street' to a main line signalbox. Nor was that situation unusual on the postwar railway. There was a desperate shortage of signalmen in many areas and existing railwaymen just did not want to become one, especially at Connington, miles out in the sticks. And so it came about that the safety of thousands of passengers was in the hands of an inexperienced 20-year-old, with one year's service.

He was finally tried on charges of manslaughter and endangering the safety of railway passengers, at the Huntingdon Autumn Assizes held at Nottingham in November and December 1968, to which he pleaded not guilty. After days and days of legal argument he took the advice of his counsel and changed his plea to guilty on a charge of unlawfully operating the signal and points mechanism of Connington South signalbox so as to endanger persons being conveyed on a railway, for which he was sentenced to two years imprisonment. The judge instructed the jury to acquit him on the charge of manslaughter. The case provided one of the very few instances on Britain's railways where a signalman has deliberately hazarded a train.

But the fates had been propitiated. The third accident had happened and everyone could relax. The ghost of Connington smiled his secret smile. Yes, there is a ghost at Connington; the area is steeped in history. But that is another story!

Below:
Deltic Co-Co No D9012 *Crepello* featured in the accident at Connington on 15 December 1961. Fully repaired for further traffic, and later renumbered 55012, this fine diesel was photographed 17 years later well off its beaten track at Armathwaite while heading the 'Thames-Forth' railtour on 20 May 1978.
Peter J. Robinson

Miracles at Colwich

Left:
On 2 October 1988 No 86244 crosses the swing nose crossing at Colwich with the 07.20 Glasgow-Euston. The locomotive front is just at the point of impact in the fateful collision which is the subject of this article.
Colin Boocock

Below:
This aerial view of part of the Colwich crash scene shows the extent of mechanical devastation. The locomotive of the southbound train, *City of Milton Keynes*, lies on its side facing north, near the crane at the top of the picture. The other locomotive is in the centre of the print, destroyed almost beyond recognition. How 835 people walked out of this scene alive was surely a miracle. *Daily Mirror*

Colin Boocock

The Minister has reported, his recommendations have been digested and the railway authorities have taken the necessary action. The collision between two InterCity trains at Colwich is already fading in memory, to take its place among the historical accidents which have influenced future railway operating and engineering practices.

Yet the Colwich crash surely deserves more than this. True, Driver Goode lost his life in the locomotive cab of No 86211, the saddest result of a dreadful day. But there is a positive side to the Colwich crash which I have never seen tabled for discussion — surely many miracles happened on that day.

To substantiate this claim, we need to imagine ourselves in the position of a passenger on the 17.20 Liverpool to London train. One has just settled down in a seat after joining the train at Stafford. People around are talking, reading, dozing or just looking out of the carriage window. It is a Friday evening, and for most people the working week is at last over. We can relax as speed reaches nearly 100mph while the train emerges from Shugborough tunnel. Then the train crashes. Our carriage swings violently to one side as it jackknifes against the one in front. People and luggage are thrown about. There is momentary pandemonium, then relative silence. Shock is setting in.

The 17.00 from Euston to Manchester Piccadilly that day was well laden, with around 400 people on board. The southbound Liverpool train was even fuller, with 435 sitting in the saloons, standing in the gangway ends or otherwise milling about. As the Manchester train, moving ever more slowly, came towards the swing nose crossing where the up line from Crewe crosses the down line to Stoke and Manchester at Colwich, the up train from Liverpool approached and hit it at around 95mph. The two Class 86s met at a combined speed of around 100mph. The southbound engine, carrying the name *City of Milton Keynes*, somersaulted over No 86429 *The Times* and landed at the side of the Up track. Driver Goode died in his cab. The '86/4' on the northbound train was pushed back at least two coach lengths from the point of impact. The leading BG on the southbound train had its frame bent double at the leading end. The first-class Mk 3 behind it emerged to slide on its side for some distance until it buried its end in an overhead structure support, bending it over. The second Mk 3, the buffet car and several Mk 2 saloons in the 17.20 from Liverpool jackknifed together on the bridge over the road through Colwich village. A further Mk 2 coach rolled over and rested against the west parapet of the bridge. Several coaches at the back ends of both trains remained on the rails. During the few seconds it took for the motion of the collision to become stilled, dust, ballast, glass and pieces of railway equipment flew about and the 25kV overhead cables came down.

Fig 2
Location of Colwich on the West Coast main line.

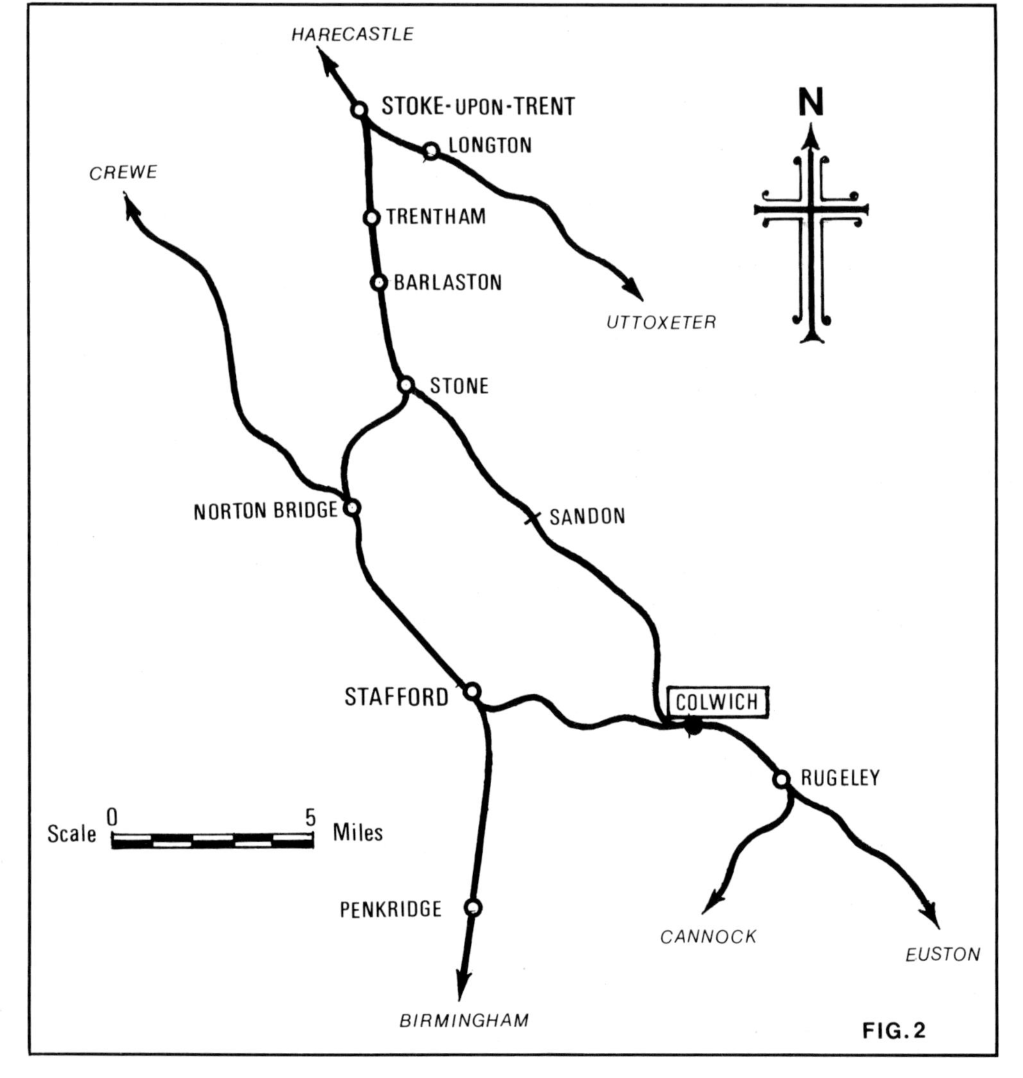

Apart from poor Driver Goode, nobody was killed. The press and railway publicity made strong and accurate claims that modern coaching stock is structurally designed to withstand this kind of impact sufficiently to protect life. This it had clearly done. At Colwich, however, I believe another force was at work.

Consider the following facts, all of which emerged during the public enquiry, or from discussions the author has had with people closely involved.

The driver and his colleague in the driving cab of the northbound train jumped out of their cab just before the impact. The spot where they landed was the only place for yards around on which no heavy debris fell. Good luck?

The guard of the Liverpool train had walked out of his BG just after leaving Stafford, to inspect tickets, and had passed through the leading first-class coach before the crash. He was really fortunate not to have been in either of the two leading vehicles. The only sizeable blocks of empty seats in the Liverpool train were in the two first-class Mk 3 coaches. This was just as well, considering what happened to these. No-one was in either of the crushed toilet compartments of the Mk 3s. Let us be thankful.

Two people sitting at a table in the

Above:
Bo-Bo No 86212 hauls a colourful formation of Network SouthEast Mk 1 stock on a Saturday morning extra service, on the down fast line approaching Colwich on 2 October 1988. *Mrs Mary Boocock*

Below:
About two months after the crash a thanksgiving and memorial service was held in the parish church at Colwich. It was broadcast nationwide. Thanks were given for the remarkable way in which all lives but one were spared on that fateful day.
Colin Boocock

Mk 1 RMB buffet car on the southbound train were catapulted to the other end of the vehicle by the impact. The table and seats from which they had just been forcibly ejected were immediately wrecked when a loose bogie frame penetrated the buffet car side. Many other railway customers were sitting or standing in the gangway ends of the jackknifed Mk 2 coaches. Surprisingly, none was thrown out. Many carriage windows were broken as the vehicles swung and rolled about: no-one fell through. What was amazing to the author was that nobody fell out to become trapped under the wreckage.

There were many, many more stories like this, hundreds in fact that are held privately, locked in individual memories. Some 835 people sat, stood or walked into positions of relative safety in these two trains before the crash took place. The probability of there being less than a dozen fatalities in such an accident must be quite low. True, a few legs were broken, one lady was unfortunate enough to loose a foot, ribs were cracked and there were many cuts and bruises. But no passenger was killed. Many said 'Praise God'. If there really was such a thing as a miracle, then Colwich had just witnessed many.

If good forces were at work during the crash, more came afterwards. At the public enquiry the signalman described the scene as the trains collided. He then added the words: 'And then the village arrived!'

Colwich is a small village set just beside the railway. Its local school backs on to the down side of the line and the church is just across the road. Help came immediately and voluntarily to relieve the stress and shock. The tragedy could not have happened at a better place. The school buildings were opened up and became a reception centre. People took shaken travellers into their houses and tended to the needs of their unexpected guests: many passengers even stayed overnight before resuming their journeys.

Even the aftermath of clearing up the damage and destruction from the crash site was made easy by the presence of the most ideal grass field from which the large cranes could work, and in which damaged carriages could be temporarily placed before being taken away for repair or scrap. The field belonged to a Christian convent situated nearby.

The villagers at Colwich did not let the matter rest at that. My wife and I joined the hundred or so who attended the memorial and thanksgiving service which was held in the village church about a month later. There were two themes at the service: sadness was entirely appropriate because a driver had lost his life in the crash; but there was thanksgiving also for the strange way in which most people had been able just to walk away from the scene that evening. There was also thanksgiving for the way in which the villagers of Colwich had been welded into a much closer, friendlier community by their collective experience that day. The service was broadcast on the BBC network. One of the programme controllers had been a passenger in the crash.

British Rail recognised the value of the efforts made by the village. When the crash site was being cleared and repaired, General Man-

Above:
The garden of remembrance at Colwich is still carefully and regularly tended. It was laid out on the spot where the locomotive of the southbound train came to rest. Replica nameplates bearing the name *City of Milton Keynes*, flank the memorial plaque. *Colin Boocock*

Below:
The 10.30 Glasgow InterCity service approaches Colwich on the down fast line, headed by new Bo-Bo No 90003. *Colin Boocock*

ager Cyril Bleasdale instructed that there was to be no debris left of any kind or size to remind anyone of the mangled mess of railway equipment that had so violently been formed that day — that the clearing and

"THEY'VE JUST RUNG UP TO ASK IF WE CAN DO ANOTHER ...... AT STRANRAER!"

tidying up was done inside four days and nights was truly an outstanding achievement. An excellent job was done shortly afterwards in replacing the fences and hedges that were damaged during the recovery operations.

Local railway staff of the civil engineer's department obtained agreement to present the village with a small garden of remembrance for the lost life of Driver Goode. This was planted where his locomotive landed, at the side of the railway near the junction. The garden is tended regularly so that, with its plaque and two replica *City of Milton Keynes* nameplates on display, it forms an attractive and permanent reminder in a positive way of the sadness and the miracles that came together on 19 September 1986.

Come, let us praise the Lord!
Let us sing for joy to God, who protects us.
Let us come before him with thanksgiving
and sing joyful songs of praise.
(Psalm 95, verses 1 and 2)

To Kemmannugundi on the Narrow Gauge

Allan C. Baker

Deep in the heart of the Mysore State of India, now known as Karnataka, about 140 miles northwest of Bangalore, lies the Visvesvaraya Iron & Steel Works. By no means the largest such establishment in India, it is, nevertheless, the largest producer of specialist alloy steels, with an installed capacity of 77,000 tonnes of such products per annum. It is also unique, certainly by western standards, in employing open hearth, LD oxygen (Linz & Donawitz), and electric furnaces simultaneously for steelmaking. The two Siemens Martin basic open hearth furnaces date from 1936 and 1943, and have a capacity of 25 tonnes each. The LD plant, consisting of two 12 tonnes converters dates from 1965, whilst the three electric arc furnaces of 20 tonnes each, date from 1965, 1967 and 1968 respectively. Iron is refined from the ore by electric pig iron furnaces, two older ones each with a capacity of 100 tonnes per day, dating from 1952 and 1955, with the later two 187.5 tonnes per day furnaces dating from 1971. The original conventional blast furnace, with a capacity of 80 tonnes per day and dating from 1918, still stands, superseded due to the difficulty in obtaining sufficient quantities of high quality coking coal or charcoal. The principle of the electric pig iron furnace was developed in Sweden and lent itself to the smelting of iron ore using low quality coke.

The works dates from 1918, but it was as long ago as 1915, when an American, C. P. Perin (of Perin & Marshall, Consulting Engineers), adviser to the Tata Iron & Steel Co, was invited by the Mysore Government to report on the iron ore resources of the State, the Mysore Geological Department having found deposits of high grade iron ore in the Baba Budan mountains. He recommended in May 1916, the construction of an ironworks near the extensive ore reserves at Bhadravati, along with a wood distillation plant for the production of charcoal pig iron, using the exten-

Below:
Bagnall and Kerr Stuart 2-8-2s pose alongside each other on the ash pits by the narrow gauge locomotive shed on the evening of 22 November 1979. The Bagnall is No 14 (2906/1950) and the other is No 41 (4241/1922). Note the difference in size.
Allan Baker

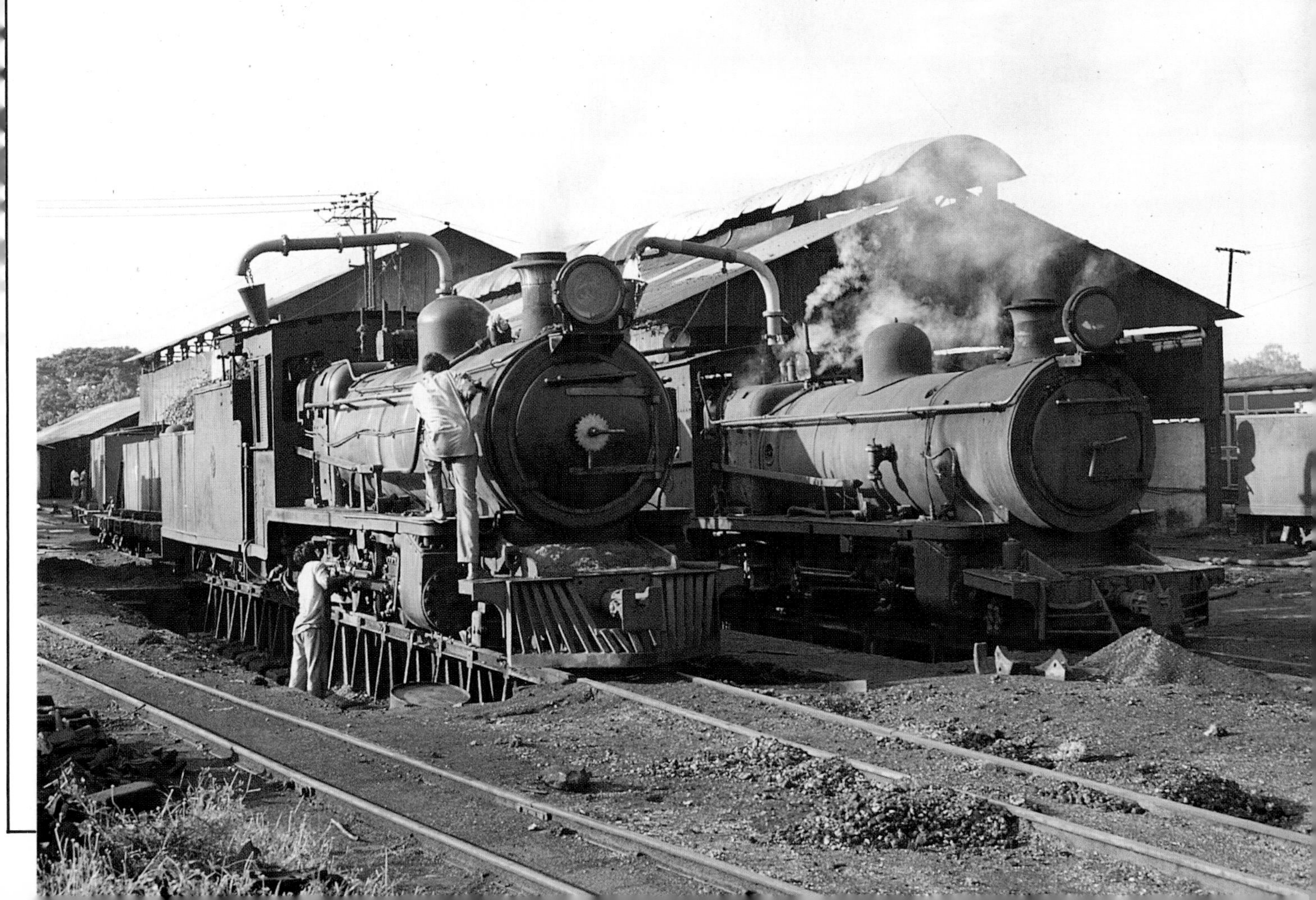

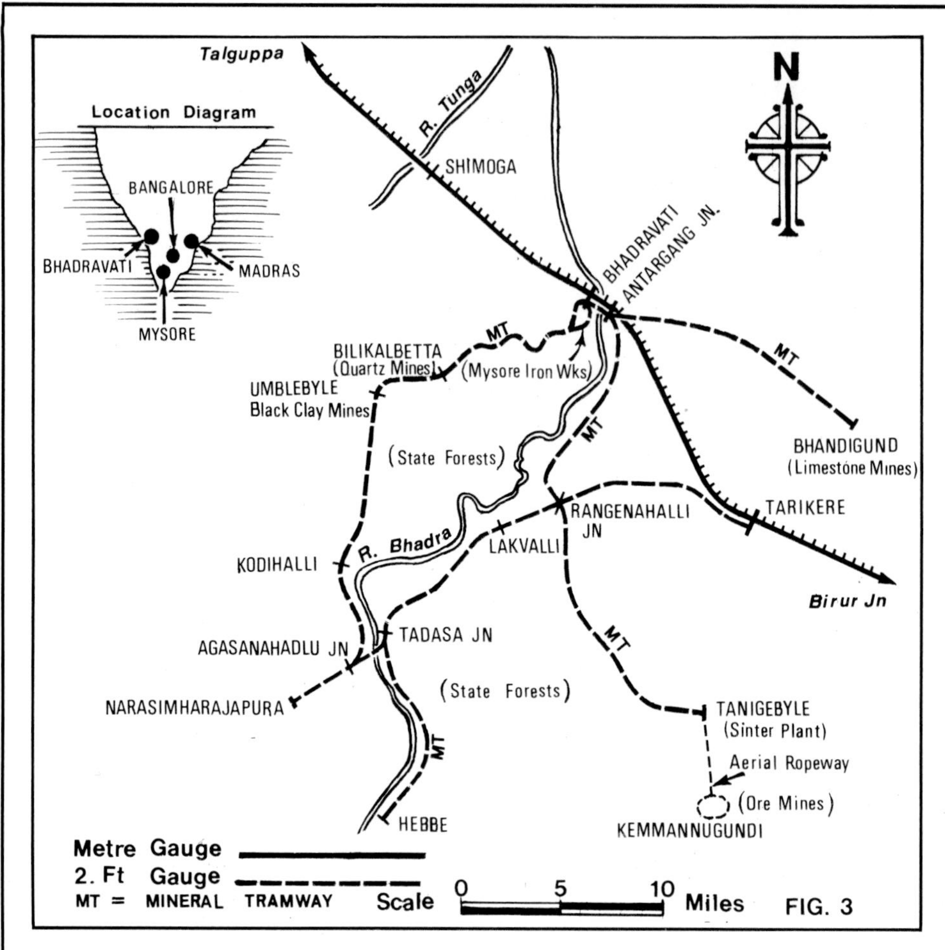

Fig 3
Railways in the area of Bhadravati, India.

sive forests to provide timber. This was sanctioned in 1917, commenced in 1918, and commissioned in 1923, the blast furnace having a capacity of 60 tonnes, increased to 80 tonnes in 1929, and for many years the only one of its kind in India. The wood distillation plant with by-product recovery units had a capacity of 200 tonnes per day.

Historical Background

The metre gauge branch line from Birur — on the Mysore State Railways main line from Mysore to Harihar — to Bhadravati, 28.4 miles, and onward to Shimoga, 11.18 miles, dates from 1 December 1899. The Bangalore-Harihar section, where end-on junction was made with the Madras & Southern Mahratta Railway (MSMR) main line north to Poona was, in fact, operated prior to 1 January 1938, by the MSMR, as indeed was the Birur-Shimoga section, prior to 1 October 1919.

To help in the development of the area west of Bhadravati, a 2ft 'tram' line was built from Tarikere, 15.53 miles from Birur, 11.88 miles due west to Lakvalli, opened 15 January 1915 (to passengers on 22 May 1915), and onwards a further 14.72 miles to Narasimharajapura on 15 May 1917. This was principally to open up the extensive forests for development, but a passenger service seems to have been operated, (one train each way per day in 1929) and the whole had been authorised in September 1913, as the Tarikere-Narasimharajapura Tramway of the Mysore State Railways system. The first locomotive came from Örenstein & Koppel in 1913, and others followed from Kerr Stuart in 1918. On 5 February 1921 a 9.60-mile branch was opened from Tadasa, about half-way between Lakvalli and Narasimharajapura, southwards to Hebbe; it was authorised in 1917 as the Tadasa-Hebbe Tramway, and never seems to have had anything but a freight sevice.

Returning now to the ironworks, the Mysore State Railways was also engaged in building lines to assist in providing the works with its other raw materials. Firstly, a 2ft gauge line was built due south, from the works 23 miles to Tanigebyle, which stands at the foot of the Baba Budan Range in the Western Ghats, on top of which, at Kemmannugundi (meaning 'red dirt' in the local language), lie extensive iron ore deposits, and where mining operations commenced in 1923. A further 2ft gauge system was built around the mines themselves, and an aerial ropeway, 2 miles long was built to bring the ore down to Tanigebyle. This line crossed on the level, but does not appear to have connected with, the Tarikere-Narasimharajapura line at Rangenhalli Junction, approximately 13 miles from Bhadravati, and 9 miles from Tarikere. Originally the ore was transported direct to the works in the state it was mined — it has a 58-60% ferrous content — but due to the large fines yield — 30% — a sintering plant was constructed at Tanigebyle, which was commissioned in 1962, with a capacity of 75,000 tonnes per annum; thus, the tramway from Bhadravati not only takes sintered ore to the works, but also, as return traffic, coke breeze for the sinter plant.

Originally, the mines were operated by a series of American locomotives (the Tata Iron & Steel Co, which remained as Managing Agents until May 1924, had a liking for American motive power in all its plants), and a series of 2-6-4 tanks came from Baldwin in 1919-20, doubtless some at least, originally working the 23-mile section between the works and Tanigebyle. By 1973, only three of the Baldwins survived at Kemmannugundi, and the narrow gauge system there was replaced by lorries the following year; only No 3 survives, 'stuffed and mounted' on a plinth at Bhadravati. All these locomotives by the way, were built to the order of the Mysore State Railways, which seem to have not only built, but also originally operated, the tramways.

Another line was built to tap further forest areas, heading due west of Bhadravati, 15 miles to Umblebyle, and later, around 1938, when a cement plant was commissioned at Bhadravati, black clay mines were opened up there to provide the principle raw material for the cement. This line originally extended southwards beyond Umblebyle, to join the Tarikere-Narasimharajapura line at a place called Agasanahadlu, just over 24 miles from Bhadravati, and a similar distance from Tarikere, but for how long a period is not clear, or for what purpose. Later, quartz mines were opened up at Bilikalbetta, around 6.25 miles from Bhadravati on the line to Umblebyle. Lastly, yet another line was built from Bhadravati, leaving the Tanigebyle line at Antargang Junction, just outside the works area, and passing under the main metre gauge line, to head 12 miles eastwards, to serve limestone mines at Bhandigund, and dating from 1934, when these mines opened.

On completion of the original project, and full commissioning of the works in 1923, a new company, the Mysore Iron Works Co, was established. With the cessation of the managing agency of the Tata company in May 1924, the government — in the form of the Mysore State Railways — ceased to be directly involved with the railways and the tramways to Tanigebyle and Umblebyle passed to the same management as the works. The construction and equipment costs of the tramways were debited to the formation of the plant.

Steel manufacture commenced in 1936, and the works changed its name to the Mysore Iron & Steel Works at that time. In 1978 the combined undertaking employed 12,300 people, covered 941 acres, and produced 180,000 tonnes of pig iron, 48,000 tonnes of mild steel, 77,000 tonnes of alloy steel, 18,000 tonnes of castings and 96,000 tonnes of cement. The trading name was changed again, this time to the Visvesvaraya Iron & Steel Ltd on 16 February 1976, the year of its golden jubilee and in commemoration of its founding Engineer, Dr M. Visvesvaraya.

In connection with a large reservoir project at Bhadra, west of Tarikere, the Mysore State Railways line to Narasimharajapura, and the branch to Hebbe were closed to public traffic in 1949, and handed over to the Public Works Department; both seem to have been closed and lifted after construction work on the reservoir was complete.

Locomotives

To operate the tramways the Mysore State Railways ordered four elegant 2-8-2 outside-cylinder tender engines from Kerr Stuart & Co Ltd, of the California Works, Stoke-on-Trent, and these were despatched as Nos 1, 2, 8 and 9, in October and November 1922. The Baldwins were Nos 3-7 and Nos 1 and 2 had been metre gauge H. K. Porter 0-4-0Ts, in a common list. Doubtless, by the time the Kerr Stuarts arrived it had been decided to have separate metre and narrow gauge numbering.

These fine machines had 12in × 18in cylinders, 2ft 5in-diameter coupled wheels and a wheelbase of 20ft 3in. Weighing 33 tons in working order they were the staple motive power until after the war. A typical design of their builder, they followed closely a series of engines built for the 2ft gauge Gwalior Light Railway (later Scindia State Railways), most of whose routes radiated around Gwalior about 200 miles south of Dheli. The earliest members of the Gwalior engines dated from 1914, but were themselves developments of earlier machines from the same builder; there was a series of very similar 4-6-4s too, for passenger working as opposed to freight.

By and large these locomotives sufficed until the postwar expansion of the plant, and the need to bring more raw materials via the tramways. Thus, on 1 November 1946 the company placed an order with the Stratford-based locomotive builder, W. G. Bagnall Ltd, for four locomotives generally similar to the Kerr Stuarts, but slightly larger and superheated. Kerr Stuart itself had ceased trading in 1930 and, although its goodwill had been acquired by Hunslet, Bagnall was an equal beneficiary due to its 'local' contacts! As works numbers 2903-6, the new locomotives had 13½in × 18in cylinders, 2ft 9in-diameter driving wheels and a total wheelbase for engine and tender of 44ft 2⅞in. The heating surface, including the superheater, was 961sq ft, and the total weight in working order for engine and tender was 58 tons, including 2,800gal of water and 2½ tons of coal in the tender. At the 180lb/sq in working pressure this gave a tractive effort at 85% of 15,210lb, and they are truly massive engines for the narrow gauge track. They were delivered in April 1950 and carried running Nos 11-14. The long time between order and delivery was due to Bagnall's large backlog of work after the war. No 10 incidentally, was a one-off Baldwin No 64349 of 1942, also a 2-8-2, noted derelict in 1973, and doubtless supplied because British builders could not promise delivery dates at the time. In January 1956 Bagnall received a repeat order, and works No 3126, running No 15, was delivered in May the following year. Costing £21,120, it was destined to be the last new steam locomotive from Bagnall's Castle Engine Works.

Riding to Bhandigund

I have visited Bhadravati twice, the first occasion in February 1978, and the second in November the following year. In February 1978, along with two friends, I travelled south from Miraj, over the South Central and Southern Railways metre gauge main lines, by the crack diesel-hauled 'Mahalaxmi Express' (204 down), alighting at Birur, junction for the branch to Bhadravati, and

Below:
Baldwin 2-6-4T No 4 (52720/1919) stands preserved outside the main office block at Bhadravati on 5 February 1978. This engine had been used at the mines at Kemmannugundi until closure of the railway there in 1973, and was part of the original motive power for the tramway. *Allan Baker*

onwards to Shimoga. It had been an 11hr, 557km journey and our motive power Class YDM4A Co-Co diesel-electric No 6280, a 1,200hp machine built by the Montreal Locomotive Works in January 1969, (works No 6022-22) which we footplated for sizeable parts of the journey. It was indeed an experience, to see the 'fireman' exchange tokens at the single line passing places where speeds were in excess of 60km/hr!

We had hoped that our train along the branch to Shimoga would have been hauled by one of the four remaining metre gauge 'HPS' class 4-6-0s, a British design dating from 1924, as they were all allocated there. Alas this was not to be, and we had to be content with one of the ubiquitous 'YP' Pacifics, No 2351 (built by Telco in 1957). However, we were treated to the sight of an 'HPS', No 31405 (Hunslet 1718 of 1933), which was the Birur Junction station pilot, and we were able to photograph it going about its duties, before our train left. Arriving at Bhadravati almost at dusk, and just in time to photograph in silhouette against the setting sun, one of the Barclay-built metre gauge works shunters in the station yard, we took a taxi to the steelworks' guest house.

Now, Indians are far from being good correspondents and, despite several letters addressed to both Bhadravati and the head office in Mysore, our arrival was completely unheralded, and nobody knew anything about us! Still no matter, it was too late to do anything about it that day, and there were rooms to be

found for us and dinner to be had. The hospitality was excellent, and the dinner magnificent, complete with copious supplies of beer. Karnataka practices prohibition, but alcohol supplies always seem to be readily available for tourists! The following morning, which was actually a Sunday, after breakfast we were taken to see the General Manager — who was in his office on the Sabbath — and who claimed to have received none of our letters, but promised to do what he could in obtaining permission for us to see

Left:
Bagnall No 11 (2903/1950) waits to return to Bhadravati at the Bhandigund limestone mines on the evening of 6 February 1978. *Allan Baker*

Above:
Alongside the sinter plant at Tanigebyle, Bagnall No 12 (2904/1950), waits as its train is loaded before the return run to Bhadravati on 23 November 1978. *Allan Baker*

Below:
No 11 is seen shunting in the limestone quarry before returning to the steelworks with a trainload of limestone on 6 February 1978. *Allan Baker*

and photograph the railways, suggesting in the meantime we enjoy ourselves as their guests. Fortunately, we had allowed a day's 'recovery time' against such an eventuality, and some recompense came after a trip along the branch line to Shimoga, where another of the 'HPS' 4-6-0s was tracked down, No 31401 acting as yard shunter there. On our return in the evening we were informed that all was in order for the following day, and after another hearty dinner — again including ample supplies of beer — we went to bed in anticipation.

The morning of 5 February dawned fine and clear, as we were taken by Jeep to the locomotive shed, a combined metre and narrow gauge affair, and integral with the workshops etc. Here we were introduced to Mr Channaveeappa, the Superindendent, Tramways, who was to be our guide for the day — and a delightful fellow he turned out to be. On the 2ft gauge we found Bagnalls Nos 11 and 14 in steam, with No 12 under repair in the shed, although they did pull it outside later for us to photograph. All the Kerr Stuarts were in evidence, but minus their running numbers, and known by the last two digits of their works numbers. Thus, Nos (42)40, (42)41 and (42)43 were in steam around the shed, No 40 leaving very soon after to take a train to Umblebyle, whilst No (42) 42 was dismantled for a heavy overhaul, its boiler having been removed from the frames. Despite being in steam, No 41 had its motion removed for running repairs, but this did not deter the splendid fellows from hauling it outside to be photographed, but it must have dismayed the fitters, because when it was pushed back in again her cranks were all over the place in relation to each other!

Also in the shed, serviceable but not in steam — subsequently also pulled outside for photography — was what appeared to be another Bagnall, numbered 16 and with a date, 1975, on its cabside. Investigations revealed that this locomotive had been built at the works using the accumulation of spare parts acquired over the years from Bagnall, including a complete boiler built in 1956. They also had a spare set of cylinders, wheelsets and many other motion parts, along with other items. Nevertheless, this was a very commendable effort, the result could not be told apart from its sisters, and the staff were extremely proud of their efforts, and rightly so.

Later in the day, after an absorbing morning around the shed and workshops, we were taken to the limestone mines at Bhandigund. Our train consisted of eight empty, bottom-discharge bogie hopper wagons and two coaches, one for us and another for an army of works police, not as we originally thought to look after our interests, but to guard the pay, for it was pay day for the workers at the mines! We had a wonderful journey with plenty of photostops, not a little footplating — the latter including some driving — and the pleasure of passing No 15 inward-bound with a train load of iron ore at Antargang Junction. Our engine was in lovely condition, and its brass work gleamed in the late afternoon sunshine. We spent an interesting hour or so at the mine watching No 11 shunt loaded wagons out of the quarry, and replace them with the empty ones we had brought; the loading operations were absorbing too, being in the hands of female labour, and completely unmechanised.

Time marched on all too quickly, but we soon began to get worried, as our companions seemed in no hurry to get back to Bhadravati, and we had to be away on the evening train to catch our overnight connection to Bangalore at Birur Junction, so as to regain our programmme after the day's 'recovery time' had elapsed. It turned out that there were problems with the payment of the wages (a shortage it was rumoured!) but we were assured by the friendly police inspector, that all would be well — but time kept passing by and it was completely dark when we eventually left. But it was worth it, because our return journey turned out to be just about the most fantastic narrow gauge trip I have ever had — and I include Darjeeling in this — and we made our way back at hair raising speed. Our coach was at the back of the train again, and the sight and sound — they have lovely twin whistles, a deep tone hooter and a shrill bell — of that magnificent big Bagnall tearing through the night, large headlamps fore and aft, twisting and turning with its long train, will stay with me for all time. It was literally pitch black, not a light anywhere except from the engine and the coaches, with the glow from the engine's fire, occasionally augmented as the firehole door was opened, or sparks were emitted from the chimney, both head and tail lamps picking out sections of the forest as the track curved; what a trip. We did the journey along the winding and twisting 12-mile route in less than half an hour, at what seemed like express speeds, our dawdling outward trip having occupied no less than 2hr! Needless to say we caught our train with sufficient time in

Below:
At Antargang Junction on 23 November 1979 stands Bagnall 2-8-2 No 12 with the train on which the author rode to the mines at Kemmannugundi. Notice the coaches at the back of the train, and two of the wagons loaded with coal breeze for the sinter plant at Tanigebyle. *Allan Baker*

hand for a wash and brush up at the guest house first, and had ample time to bid a just farewell to our new found friends.

By train to Kemmannugundi

So tempted had we been by this visit, that we vowed to return to this wonderful place, and this we achieved the following year, arriving on the evening of Wednesday 21 November 1979, again by the late afternoon train from Birur; on this occasion having journeyed north from Mysore. Yet again, surprise, surprise, our correspondence had gone unanswered, and nobody knew we were coming. However, we took a taxi to the guest house, where we were treated like old friends, addressed by name, and presented with a corrected account from the previous year, which still had a few Rupees oustanding, and which the friendly clerk seemed more happy about finalising, and correcting his books, than actually seeing us! Nevertheless, the hospitality was as good as before, and we were assured that all would be in order on the morrow.

Once again we were taken after breakfast to see the Manager, a different fellow this time, indeed we saw nobody we recognised, except that is, for the guest house clerk! True to predictions the Manager knew nothing of our visit, but offered to have us escorted around the works site while he tried to sort it out, but until he did so, *no* photographs. Despite his grandiose title, he had to have government permission before we could take photographs. If only we had written in advance . . . However, we were treated to a wonderful tour around the whole works, and it was truly amazing to be able to see no less than three different methods of making steel on one site. Fortunately, with the experience of the previous year in mind, we had allowed some 'recovery time', because we were anxious to have a trip along one of the other tramways, preferably that to the ironstone mines at Kemmannugundi.

Well, authority came in the late afternoon, which allowed us to take advantage of the best light of the day, taking photographs around the locomotive shed and works, as the engines came home to rest after their day's work. Arrangements were also made for our trip to the mines the following day; nothing was too much trouble. After yet another night's splendid entertainment, and the beer was still in good supply, we set off the next morning in the company of Mr M. V. Sreenivasan, Deputy Manager, Internal Traffic, and Mr Venkatesh, Deputy General Manager, Railways; do not ask me how these two apportioned their duties, but they were great guys, and with them just about everything was possible. We had Bagnall No 12 this time, along with seven bogie hopper wagons, of which two were loaded with coke breeze for the sinter plant at Tanigebyle, and attached at the rear was the normal bogie coach which seemed to accompany all trains, although who the passengers were supposed to be was less clear, and an inspection saloon specially for us. This rather fine vehicle was extremely will appointed, and complete with valet to look after our every need, having been built by the Gloucester Carriage & Wagon Co over 60 years earlier, and reputed to have originally been for the use of the Maharajah of Mysore. Be that as it may, it was extremely comfortable and normally reserved for very special guests! Once again we had a very interesting trip, with photostops, footplating, and on this occasion lunch aboard.

Above:
Bagnall No 11 threading through the forest areas en route to Kemmannugundi on 23 November 1979. *Allan Baker*

On arrival at Tanigebyle we were able to watch the process of loading the wagons from the massive hopper at the sinter plant, and the train being re-formed for its return journey. Next we were taken by Jeep up on to the hillside to see the mining operations at Kemmannugundi itself, 4,668ft above sea level, where again the loading operations were mainly in the hands of women and with no labour saving devices at all. The aerial ropeway to the sinter plant was inspected, and we saw the remains of the railway system that was used before the advent of the large dumper trucks. Afterwards we spent the remainder of the afternoon exploring with our companions all number of interesting places in the vicinity, returning to Bhadravati in the evening direct by Jeep.

So ended the second, and, as events have turned out, the last, of my trips to this fascinating backwater of Indian industry. India is indeed a wonderful country, and the hospitality second to none once official clearance is obtained — they just could not do enough for us. Most unfortunately as I pen these words, news comes that a November 1987 visitor found all tramway operations ceased, the Kerr Stuarts being very much out of use, but the Bagnalls stored, albeit supposedly serviceable. Doubtless spare part problems have had a bearing on the decision to close the tramways, and this had been mentioned on my visits, and I can only presume that the local roads have been improved sufficiently to allow the dumper trucks to bring the raw materials direct to the works. A great pity, and so ends another outpost of British steam, and so far away from the mother country.

In conclusion, I would like specially to thank Hugh Hughes, for all his help, assistance and wise counsel in the compilation of this article.

Photo Feature:

Severn Valley variety

Hugh Ballantyne

The Severn Valley Railway has established itself as one of Britain's leading preserved railways. One of the reasons for this is the variety of motive power it can call on for its services at any one time.

Above:
A useful locomotive for any preserved railway is the Ivatt 2-6-0 design, or its 2-6-2T equivalent, being small, economical, and strong for its size. Here, 2-6-0 No 46443 crosses Victoria Bridge on the SVR with the 4.25pm from Kidderminster to Bridgnorth. *Hugh Ballantyne*

Above right:
Decked out in early BR colours, the 4.42pm local service from Highley to Bewdley passes over Victoria Bridge behind 'Jinty' 0-6-0T No 47383 on 28 September 1985. *Hugh Ballantyne*

Right:
A feature of the Severn Valley Railway is the number of visiting locomotives it attracts. During 1987 the Midland Railway Centre's Somerset & Dorset Railway Class 7F 2-8-0 was on the SVR. It was photographed at Oldbury with the 11.35 from Bridgnorth to Kidderminster on 17 October. *Hugh Ballantyne*

53809
53809

The rebuilt 'Merchant Navy' class: Britain's finest Pacifics?

Colin Boocock

It is a natural thing that the locomotives one grew up with are appreciated more than those on other people's railways. Crewe men, for example, still wax lyrical about the Stanier Pacifics. Doncaster folk would put their money on an 'A4' 4-6-2 in any race. Swindonians are proud of their 'King' heritage.

Men of the Southern liked the 'Merchant Navy' Pacifics even before they were rebuilt. The engines 'could pull anything', the fireboxes 'would burn anything'. That they burned too much coal, used too much water, and were 'light on their feet' could not suppress appreciation of the outstanding haulage achievements of these modern machines. When the 1948 locomotive exchanges were mooted, the 'Merchant Navy' 4-6-2s were entered with confidence, though with some diffidence about their thermal efficiency.

The Chief Mechanical Engineer of the Southern Railway, O. V. S. Bulleid, had provided the Southern with 20 4-6-2s 'of the most modern design' for working heavy trains over the most demanding routes, to Exeter, to Bournemouth and Weymouth and to Dover. All of these routes included severe gradients, particularly those to Exeter and Dover, and train loadings were usually heavy. While most Southern expresses were limited by platform lengths to around 13 coaches, the 'Bournemouth Belle's' set of heavy, 12-wheeled Pullman cars tared over 500 tons, the 'Atlantic Coast Express' had to mount the 1 in 75 of Honiton Bank, and the 'Night Ferry' could load to over 15 vehicles. All had to be pathed through the Southern's briskly-run electrified suburban area.

Bulleid's 'Merchant Navy' class answered the needs of the Southern Railway so well that a further 10 examples were ordered. They were delivered in 1948 and 1949, after nationalisation.

The engines had been designed for high performance but low weight. (In both these aspects Bulleid had succeeded, though the high performance had been bought at a price.) To reduce frame stresses the main frame plates were closer together, central with the axlebox horn guides (this feature was also adopted on BR's excellent Class 9F 2-10-0s). The boiler was of large diameter with tapered barrel containing no fewer than 40 superheater flues and elements (a record at the time?) and the tube length was short enough not to restrict gas flow unduly. The firegrate, at 50sq ft, was very large by British standards. The firebox was of welded steel, not the usual riveted copper, and required controlled water treatment to avoid corrosion, but proved to be an excellent and easily repairable choice. It was fitted with two thermic syphons for improved water circulation. Steam entry and exhaust pipes and passages were generously dimensioned, and a five-jet blastpipe was fitted to minimise back-pressure and maximise draught within the very tight British loading gauge.

Features aimed at reducing the locomotive weight included the chain-driven miniature valve gear with its rocker levers to magnify movement to the valve throw required; light plate smokebox and chimney construction; thin gauge plate 'air-smoothed' casing over the boiler and smokebox (which eliminated the need for traditional boiler

Left:
No 35010 *Blue Star*, one of the first 10 'Merchant Navy' locomotives, in unrebuilt form, passes Eastleigh with the down 'Royal Wessex' on 3 July 1956. This train had portions for Bournemouth West, Swanage and Weymouth. The first 10 'Merchant Navies' visually differed from the later locomotives (before rebuilding) in the angle of the front casing above and in front of the cylinders, and also in the extended casings at the top of the tender. *Colin Boocock*

Above:
The valve gear for the left side outside cylinder of the first rebuilt locomotive, No 35018, seen before it entered service. Note the similarity of the valve gear components and fixings to those used on the BR Standard 2-6-4Ts (also designed at Brighton). The slide bars are original Bulleid. The radius rod drives the combination lever below the valve rod, to compensate for the use of outside admission. *Colin Boocock*

lagging plates, running boards, brackets and valances); light plate cab skinning; and all-welded tender construction, the last 10 of which were able to tank 6,000gal of water on a three-axle frame!

Even the reduction in driving wheel diameter to 6ft 2in from the more normal 6ft 6in-6ft 9in for high speed locomotives was aimed at keeping weight down, as was the fabricated 'box-pok' construction of the wheel centres. To compensate for potentially high piston speeds, the piston stroke was reduced to 24in, instead of the more normal 26in or 28in of British practice.

With an official line maximum of 85mph the 'Merchant Navy' class engines were not restrained by their 6ft 2in wheels. Indeed, on many occasions, train performance enthusiasts timed these locomotives hauling heavy trains at up to 100mph. The highest published authenticated speed recalled by the author was 104mph. Indeed, drivers would comment that the engines could run freely at speed with the steam reverser set at 25% cut-off and the regulator only a little open. This apparent free running on a 'light rein' was totally inconsistent with the high water and coal consumptions which were a feature of these engines.

Under British Railways' auspices the maintenance schedules for steam locomotives were brought into a standard (former LMS) pattern, and costings were recorded against the various classes. Generally, maintenance costs per mile were seen to be higher for bigger engines (not surprisingly), for more complex engines, and for engines which exhibited unreliability. The 'Merchant Navy' class scored high on all three counts. Their overhaul interval (around 65,000 miles between intermediate repairs) was not excessive for prewar engines but compared poorly with the postwar products of the LMS.

The high fuel consumption of the 'Merchant Navy' was explained following a series of controlled tests on the Rugby test plant and over the Settle-Carlisle line. There were two principal adverse features at work. One was the valve gear, which failed to produce consistent and accurate valve events. The effects of the chain drive to the valve gear were to delay valve events when the chain was slack, and to vary them as the chain took up different positions dynamically as speed increased. At high speed, when the steam reverser was set at 25%, actual cut-offs were around 40%, a very uneconomical way of handling a steam locomotive. Drivers compensated for this high actual cut-off by partially closing the regulator, so gaining the impression that the engines would run 'on a whisp of steam'. The opposite was actually the case!

Valve events were also inaccurate because any wear in the valve gear pins and links was multiplied by the rocking levers, and the steam reverser was unable to place and hold the setting accurately at a fixed cut-off.

All this led to high steam consumption relative to the power output. To produce this higher steam volume the fireman had to feed more coal to the firegrate. Another feature was at work which increased coal consumption marginally still further. The relatively crude section of the fabricated 'dustbin' chimney and petticoat did not provide a smooth passage for the exhaust jets, there being angular joints where the rolled plates were welded together. This gave rise to turbulence and was said to be responsible for incomplete combustion of the coal.

Leakage of lubricating oil from the oilbath in which the valve gear operated was chronic, at an average use of a gallon of oil per 100 miles run. An offshoot of this was that oil was said to get on to the wheel treads, and so reduce the already limited adhesion of these locomotives, which frequently slipped on starting.

With all these problems the reader may be forgiven for being surprised that the 'Merchant Navy' class

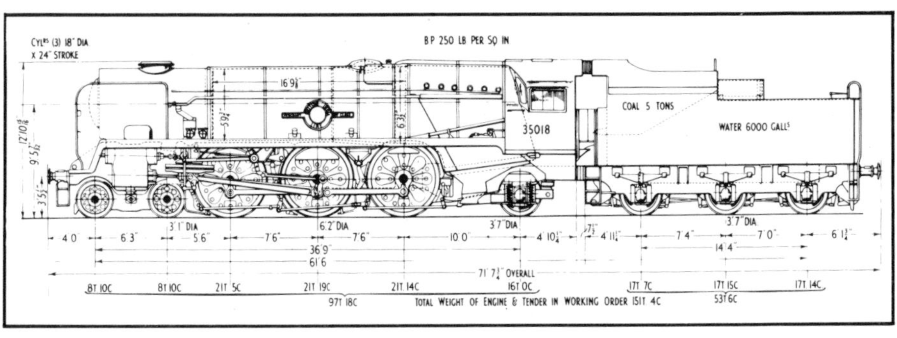

Fig 4
Diagram of rebuilt 'Merchant Navy' class locomotive.

locomotives were adored by many and were suffered amiably by the majority who knew them. The reasons for this lay in their dominant, redeeming features. They almost never ran short of steam. They could always time a train, given barely half a chance. They were easy to fire from a skill point of view, even if more coal was burned than seemed reasonable. They rode well and ran well. And they looked good!

But economics hold a very firm grip on life, and the decision to rebuild the locomotives to remove their unsatisfactory and expensive features became almost inevitable. The design work and the technical inspiration came from the Southern Region's drawing office at Brighton under the general direction of Ron Jarvis. The influence of R. A. Riddles, British Railways' chief of mechanical engineering, was evident in the selective use of BR standard component design and in the styling of the rebuilt locomotives.

The rebuilding retained the successful key components which gave credit to Bulleid's designs: the main frames, boiler, bogie, pony truck and wheels were retained as were the outside cylinders and the tender. The chain driven valve gear and its oilbath were removed, together with the steam reverser, as were the fabricated smokebox and chimney. The aim of the revised design was to fit conventional Walschaerts' valve gear in three independent sets to improve efficiency, and modify the action of the smokebox, chimney and petticoat on the exhaust gases to improve combustion.

To fit a set of conventional inside valve gear was not possible with the original cylinder design, so a new inside cylinder was fitted. This had a suitably offset valve chest, and was designed for inside admission to reduce the possibility of problems with steam glands in inaccessible places. Retaining the outside cylinders meant that the rebuilt locomotives had a mixture of inside and outside steam admission, a feature responsible in part for their syncopated beat. In front of the inside cylinder was a new fabricated frame stretcher combined with a rigid smokebox saddle.

New crank axle balance weights were fitted which provided full dynamic balancing. (Bulleid had claimed it was only necessary to balance reciprocating components

Left:
About 30 years ago, newly rebuilt 'Merchant Navy' Pacific No 35027 *Port Line* stands outside Eastleigh works. The splendid amalgamation of BR standard features (the smoke deflectors and valances for example) with the original Bulleid style (wheels; cab and tender profiles) gave these locomotives a unique and particularly handsome aspect. *B. J. Swain*

Below left:
No 35008 *Orient Line* takes the up 'Bournemouth Belle' Pullman train past Shawford in 1964. *B. J. Swain*

Bottom left:
Rounding the curve and about to dive under the Worting flyover west of Basingstoke is No 35029 *Ellerman Lines* with an express from Waterloo to the west of England in 1964. This locomotive is now sectioned in the National Railway Museum at York. *B. J. Swain*

Bottom:
Thundering past Shawford at speed is No 35008 with a Waterloo-Bournemouth express. *B. J. Swain*

since the three-cylinder layout was theoretically self-balancing.) The engines received new cast steel axleboxes with bronze bearing inserts in place of their former solid bronze ones. The new axleboxes had manganese steel horn linings to reduce wear and so enable shopping periods to be extended.

The outside valve gear was BR standard in layout, except that the top two pins of the combination lever were in reverse positions and the angle of the return crank was also reversed, so as to operate the piston valves in the correct sequence for outside admission cylinders.

The new smokebox was a welded steel barrel, being riveted directly to the front tubeplate flange, so that its outside diameter would be less than that of the boiler lagging plates (a feature also of the 'WD' 2-8-0s and the '9Fs'). The five-jet Lemaître blastpipe was retained, but lined up with a properly shaped and coned cast iron chimney and petticoat, the chimney having the BR standard 'Horwich' lip around the rim. Unusually, but logically in view of the very wide superheater header to which access would be required, the original oval smokebox door was retained, giving the rebuilds a distinctive frontal appearance.

The exterior of the locomotives was finished off with conventional boiler lagging and cladding. BR standard running boards and valances were fitted, lower in height from the rail than on large BR Standard locomotives. The bottom of the cabside sheets was raised to conform with the general styling, and BR standard 'LNER' style full depth smoke deflectors were mounted each side of the smokebox. Painted Brunswick green, fully lined out and varnished, and reunited with its tender, a rebuilt 'Merchant Navy' was a most impressive looking machine.

The question remained: 'Will they perform?' No 35018 *British India Line* failed on its first two trial runs on passenger trains because the piston valve rod gland clearance was too tight for the heat of outside admission valves. This was quickly corrected, and the early locomotives settled down to front line duties such as the 'Bournemouth Belle' and 'Royal Wessex'.

At first, drivers tried to handle the

rebuilt engines in the same manner as the unrebuilt ones. They said the rebuilt locomotives were not so free running, but that they were much more economical on coal and water. These initial comments can easily be explained.

Now that the piston valves were driven by three sets of Walschaerts gear, not given to overrunning and held in position by a good screw reverser, 25% cut-off as indicated meant just that. Drivers soon found that they had to open the regulator wider at speed. This was ideal, because the locomotives were now running with high steamchest pressures and low cut-offs, the right combination for economical running at speed. Also, the valve events were as even as could be attained with engines with mixed inside and outside admission and with the inside cylinder at a different angle to rail than the outside cylinders. Thus, steam admission and release were better controlled, and fuel consumption was lower for the same power output.

Once drivers became used to the rebuilt engines reports began to come in that the locomotives could run every bit as freely as before. Indeed, 104mph appears to have been reached by a rebuild also!

Some observations of these locomotives in service are interesting. They were certainly more surefooted than the unrebuilt locomotives. The reasons for this are more likely to be that the valves were properly adjusted and timed, and that the new regulator was easier to control, than the oft-quoted one about oil on the wheel treads of the unrebuilt engines.

There is no doubt that coal and water consumption were reduced in every day running. More complete combustion, together with the most effective use of the steam, combined to ensure fuel economy. On several occasions the author saw a rebuilt 'Merchant Navy' with a 5,100gal tender take a heavy Sunday evening train nonstop from Bournemouth to Waterloo. With the unrebuilt engines, drivers would normally only try this if their mount had a 6,000gal tender, and more usually they would stop at Southampton to take water.

Drivers commented that the rebuilds rode less smoothly than the original engines. Several changes would have combined to cause this, so the comment is not surprising. What is surprising is that the difference was not more marked. The engines had already received stronger coupled wheel springs. The valve gear on the rebuilds was much heavier than before, and full dynamic balancing had been added (in the author's opinion the most serious influence on ride). The author recalls vividly the different effects of hearing rebuilt and unrebuilt engines passing his office at Eastleigh at speed. There was no doubt in his mind that the rebuilt engines inflicted a much more prominent hammer blow to the ground than did the unrebuilt locomotives. It may be that Bulleid had been right after all!

Later in the life of these excellent locomotives the author, while working as a technical assistant at Brighton, had the task of assembling data to show whether the rebuilding had been a good investment, and whether the work had achieved the planned savings. He obtained coal consumption figures from the motive power department which showed the average coal used per mile was certainly less on the rebuilt engines. The mileages which the rebuilds ran between planned works repairs were considerably higher, approaching 90,000 miles on average, and in this and depot maintenance costs came some very useful technical cost savings. When all the figures were summarised they showed a payback on the investment in around five years. While all this now comes from memory, there is no doubt at all that the case was proven for the 'Merchant Navy' class. (For the lighter Pacifics, many of which had a short life in their rebuilt condition, the case was distinctly marginal, but that is another story.)

So the rebuilding had paid for itself, and the Southern Region had been provided with a Pacific class of power group 8P which was surely a match for any other. Maybe they were not intended to be as fast as an 'A4', nor had they to pull such weighty trains as did the 'Duchesses', but they were the equals of all of them in day-to-day running, reliability and effectiveness, and better than each of them in at least one of these attributes. And remember they were at least 5 tons lighter than any of them!

The author finds it quite surprising that so few of Bulleid's technical innovations were applied to the BR Standard locomotive designs, all of which postdated his Pacifics. Apart from the '9F' 2-10-0 frames and the general dimensions of the Class 7 'Britannia' boiler (which broadly resembled the 'West Country' boiler), little of the goodness which O. V. S. Bulleid built into his engines was taken on by BR in its own designs.

For example, the steel fireboxes on the Bulleid Pacifics proved to be an excellent investment. Their ease of repair, by welding, coupled to carefully controlled water treatment, led to a number of the spare fireboxes

Below:
Both before and after rebuilding, No 35022 *Holland America Line* was a star performer. It poses at Nine Elms depot on 24 October 1959 after bringing the morning's 'Royal Wessex' to Waterloo from Weymouth. *Colin Boocock*

Above:
After rebuilding, No 35018 worked for many months as Nine Elms' star engine on the 'Bournemouth Belle' diagram. Here it is powering up Pokesdown bank with the Pullman on 2 April 1956. *Colin Boocock*

Above right:
No 35027 *Port Line*, now preserved, starts the 2.30pm from Waterloo to Bournemouth out of Southampton Central on 25 May 1957. *Colin Boocock*

which were held at Eastleigh works never being used in a locomotive!

Southern drivers criticised the BR Standard Class 5 4-6-0s (which replaced the 'King Arthurs' on the Bournemouth line) in two aspects. The crews missed having the advantages of Bulleid's electric lighting, supplied on his Pacifics by a steam driven turbo-generator. The drivers also complained about the poor view backwards past the later BR Standard tenders: on a SR Pacific there was always a line of view past the narrow coal bunker, made better when the tender side sheets were cut down in the 1950s.

The final accolade must surely go to the superb appearance of the 'Merchant Navy', rebuilds. There are not many steam locomotives which the author has admired consistently as potential works of art. Herr Gölsdorf's Austrian 2-6-4 perhaps, Ireland's GNR Compound 4-4-0s certainly, the SNCF '231D' class of the Region Ouest: all these spring to mind as beautiful in their own way. In the case of the 'Merchant Navy' locomotives, their neat front end shape, the gentle curve of the cab and tender sides, the low running board with its deep valances, and that superb nameplate, all these features combined to give the rebuilt 'Merchant Navy' class its unique appearance. Combined with the locomotives' excellent performance, carried out with relatively quiet competence, the appeal of this class can be understood.

It was quite fitting therefore that the rebuilt 'Merchant Navy' 4-6-2s should be among the locomotives hauling trains on Britain's last steam worked main line, the Waterloo-Weymouth line. Electrification to Bournemouth brought the commercial working life of these magnificent locomotives to an end in July 1967.

One can only express delight that a number of the class have since been preserved. The exploits on the main line of restored No 35028 *Clan Line* are already legendary. 1988 saw the return to public view of its colleague, No 35027 *Port Line*. The first rebuild, No 35018 *British India Line*, may well be running on the Mid-Hants Railway soon after this article appears in print. The one seen by the most people, no doubt, is No 35029 *Ellerman Lines*, whose cleverly sectioned form graces the National Railway Museum at York. There are, of course other rebuilt 'Merchant Navy' class engines which have been rescued from the scrapyard at Barry Docks, and which hopefully may yet be seen fully restored in the future.

To understand why the author believes this class to be the 'best of British' Pacifics, the reader is recommended to take a long look at No 35029 at the National Railway Museum. Observe the sheer size of the live and exhaust steam passages, the massiveness of the firebox, the huge superheater, and the good proportions of the boiler barrel itself. Watch the action of the piston valves in uncovering the steam and exhaust ports — note the large diameter of the steam chests. Imagine the sheer volume of exhaust gases that can escape through that enormous petticoat and chimney and understand how well that system was able to pull the air supply through the burning coal on the firebed. See how cleverly the weight has been kept down by use of fabricated steel structures where other engines used castings, notably in the case of frame stretchers and the coupled wheel discs. Get a feel for the driver's stance in the cab. The accessibility of the controls for the driver to reach easily from this seat was quite a new thing when Bulleid came to the Southern.

And then go and experience a preserved Bulleid Pacific in action on one of Britain's excellent working steam railways. If after that you are not convinced . . . But by then you will be!

Above:
56001 rumbles through the Wylye valley at Sherrington with an Amey Roadstone train from Whatley to Fareham on 8 December 1987.
Nick Bartlett

Below:
58034 leans to the curve near Tackley on 26 June 1986 with a train of HAA coal wagons bound for Didcot power station. *Nick Bartlett*

Photo feature:

Modern Freight on BR

There is something impressive about a block freight train thundering past with 20 or so identical wagons. Equally fascinating is the colour and variety of containers carried on Freightliner trains, or the odd mixtures of wagon types which make up the consist of the average Speedlink train.

Top:
Another coal train of merry-go-round (MGR) hopper wagons crosses the River Weaver at Frodsham westbound behind Class 20s Nos 20032 and 20055 on 23 September 1987. *Hugh Ballantyne*

Above:
Refurbished No 37674 brings an up ECC china clay train east of Brownqueen tunnel, Bodmin Parkway, on 4 May 1988. *Hugh Ballantyne*

The G&Q steams on: Update on the railways of Ecuador

Gil Hughes

In the half light of 6.25am, Baldwin 2-6-0 No 11 prepares to urge its small train from rest. Steam issues past a slightly leaking packing gland, and vapour rises from around the cylinders and wheels, as the steam blends with the damp air of a drizzling Guayaquil morning. Two or three dull chimes are heard as the driving wheels slip while the locomotive struggles for grip, but then with invisible, almost magical, might, the train is asserted into motion, and the sharp exhaust assaults the otherwise tranquil scene. As though reluctantly, a water tanker, two boxcars and two passenger carriages which form the train, emerge from the gloom of the old wooden station building of Duran, Guayaquil's rail terminus. The Friday 'Mixto' is underway, along the single track, headed east from the Pacific Coast, up to the Andes.

The train weaves past a few dwellings, and an all-concrete high-rise cemetery (very common in Latin America), passing some corroded hulks of long-since derelict locomotives, daubed with political slogans and propaganda.

After a short while, the chime whistle is sounded profoundly, along with the boiler-mounted bell; the crew of three (boiler attendant, driver, and lookout, the latter employed to keep vigil whilst standing on the oil-bunker) concentrate all their attention as the train approaches the open crossing of the main road from Guayaquil to Quito and Cuenca. The last few cars and trucks dash past in a defiant, perhaps macho, demonstration, that the train's purpose in life is less important than their own, but finally a battered bus pulls up with a squeal, and other vehicles from both directions finally condescend to follow suit.

With whistle and bell now sounding continuously, the train decisively treads it way across the wet main road, issuing its oily black smoke against the rain-filled sky.

Above:
Baldwin 2-6-0 No 11 arrives at Bucay on 15 January 1985, having just shunted off the bogie water tank (which promptly derailed itself!). *Gil Hughes*

The tough red Mogul energetically works the first stage of its journey towards the small town of Yaguachi.

The Guayaquil-Quito railway (the G & Q, often referred to as the 'good and quick'), was completed in 1908, and was founded by President Eloy Alfaro, who is sometimes referred to as the railway's only true friend from then until now. When inaugurated, it cut the journey time from the seaport of Guayaquil, to the capital, Quito, up in the Andes, from some 14 days, to about as many hours. (Not that the G&Q was Equador's first railway. The first locomotives were imported at the time of President Garcia Moreno in 1899 for the Oro Province, but that is another story.)

The present 3ft 6in gauge single-track railway spans from Guayaquil, via Bucay, Sibambe, Riobamba to Quito, and then on to Ibarra and San Lorenzo in the northernmost seaboard tip of Ecuador. A branch from Sibambe also serves the city of Cuenca. Lines also once existed between Guayaquil (central) and Salinas, (now a popular Pacific sea resort), and from Quito to Chone/Bahia (Bahia de Caráquez); these were closed in 1960 and 1967 respectively.

In addition, the service from Quito

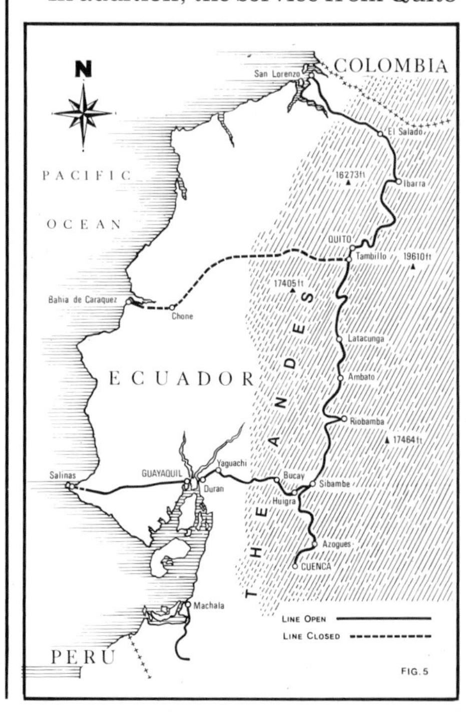

Fig 5
Northwest Ecuador, showing rail routes.

to Ibarra was suspended around 1980, but the little-known service from Ibarra to San Lorenzo still survives and the railway workshops at Ibarra are extremely active. Currently there is a total of 964km of 3ft 6in gauge track in Ecuador.

The 'Mixto' normally refers to a locomotive-hauled train, such as that described for No 11. There are also railbuses known as Autoferros, which carry the greater percentage of Ecuador's passenger traffic.

From Yaguachi, No 11 will call at Milagro for a water stop, after which it will ply up the centre of the High Street to the station, to take on passengers and freight, then on to Naranjito, cutting its normal journey short at Bucay, at the foot of the Andean highlands. (There are numerous smaller intermediate stops between those mentioned, a total of 14 between Duran and Bucay.)

Normally the 2-6-0 would be taken off to work the 13.00 train back to Duran; and the section of train destined for Riobamba would be handled by an Alco Co-Co diesel-electric. But not since late in 1982 has the G&Q been able to send a train the entire distance up the famous steep Nariz del Diablo (Devil's Nose), a series of steep switchbacks with an average gradient of 1 in 18. Severe floods caused the River Chanchan, which runs parallel with the railway, to overflow its banks, which in turn has devastated several kilometres of track, completely destroying the 150-metre long Shucos Bridge situated between Alausi and Tixan, and washing out some sections between Bucay and Huigra, It is hoped that the small section between Bucay and Naranjapata will be restored early this year (1988).

Although restoration started at once; more storms and floods in March 1986 caused further serious setbacks. The severe earthquake in March 1987 in which it is believed some 4,000 people died, and about 100,000 were made homeless, was a further blow to Ecuador's already delicate economy. Although no part of the G&Q was affected directly (the earthquake centre was in Napo Province in the northeast), the oil pipeline to the north was destroyed, cutting off Ecuador's principal export for nearly six months, resulting in many of Ecuador's projects, including reconstruction of the railway, being delayed. The story at the east side of the Nariz del Diablo is however far from happy; civil engineers have determined that the terrain at the washed-out Shucos Bridge cannot allow it to be rebuilt at that location. The problem had long-since been referred to the experts of the *Ministerio de Obras Publicas* (akin to the former British Ministry of Public Buildings and works), to seek a solution to this grave crisis. A considerable detour will be necessary, and work is in hand to seek a new route. The ENFE, (Empresa Nacional de Ferrocarriles Ecuatorianos, to give Ecuador's railway its proper title) is patiently awaiting the outcome of the Civil Engineer's studies.

Meanwhile, No 11 makes its start from Milagro, and with much whistle-blowing and bell-ringing, peruses the central reservation of the High Street, traffic dashing across the track in its normal dangerous manner. I recall leaving Milagro some years back when a little brown pick-up truck stalled whilst straddled across the rails some 50yd ahead. Although the train goes at no great speed, an emergency stop was necessary, with driving wheels locked and skidding Hollywood-fashion, before the truck driver, praying earnestly on the one hand, and cursing the entire Japanese car industry on the other, just managed to start his vehicle and drive off in the nick of time. Today however, we have only the rain to contend with. As a visitor to the footplate, it is necessary to either sit on the warm oil-bunker; (the fuel oil is steam-heated not only to allow it to flow, but to ensure correct burning); alternatively you can stand on the bunker with the look-out, (who by now is quite saturated), or, possibly more comfortably, (the expression being relative), you can stand on the flap between the locomotive and the tender, just behind the fireman, who incidentally is comfortably seated, as is the driver. From around the cast iron firedoor bright yellow flames occasionally leap out at foot level. It is a curious sensation, one's left side quite soaked, but right troused leg and shoe quite close to combustion point, leaning out obliviously, fascinated only by the intricate harmonious motions of No 11's Walschaerts valve gear.

The final climb to Bucay is quite steep, and the locomotive exhaust which has penetrated the peace between the plush rows of banana trees, pineapple fields, or sugar cane, all of which are enjoying the warm and unceasing rain, now becomes sharper as we tackle a spot of 1 in 40 on the final leg to Bucay.

The somewhat dismal, and eerily quiet town of Bucay is dominated by the railway depot, whose fitting staff cheerfully take on both steam and diesel maintenance, in parallel with their counterparts at Duran, Riobamba and Quito. However, the 1982 severing of the line has caused

Below:
A lineup of ENFE motive power at Bucay, including 2-6-0 No 11 (left) and three 2-8-0s. *Gil Hughes*

Above
G&Q 2-8-0 No 15 is a static museum display in National Unity Street, Riobamba, Ecuador. *Gil Hughes*

Below:
In Bucay shed on 15 January 1988 stands 2-8-0 No 45. The asbestos roof of the shed had recently been removed and was later to be renewed. *Gil Hughes*

Above:
Alsthom articulated diesel locomotive No 151 stands outside the workshops at Ibarra, which is on the Ibarra to San Lorenzo section of Ecuador Railways.
Gil Hughes

added problems, in that some of the rolling stock has been left stranded from any maintenance centre.

There are currently 11 oil-burning steam locomotives either in service, or capable of being returned to service. The Alco 1,250hp diesel-electric Co-Co locomotives (fabricated in Spain) are extremely capable machines, normally entrusted to climb the Nariz del Diablo instead of Baldwin 2-8-0 types. However, the original complement of 10 Alcos has, through wear and tear, and the ravages of the G&Q's rough tracks, been reduced to two or three.

One fairly simple problem is that there are insufficient stocks of steel tyres. Thin tyres, as in a road vehicle, are dangerous, and in some cases it is said that ground clearances have become reduced to an unacceptable level. However, this is just one of the difficulties with the Alco locomotives; there are also many electrical problems. A significant problem is that spares have to be imported, and payments made in US dollars. The ENFE relies for less than 10% of its revenue on its receipts, the Government providing the balance. With so many crises at one time, the import of spares has been deferred. Since the raw materials, machinery, staff, expertise, and above all, enthusiasm, still exist for maintenance of steam locomotives, for a time at least, Ecuador has almost abandoned the diesel in favour of steam. The magnitude of tasks that the railway workshops take on, particularly at Duran, are remarkable; in some cases locomotives are recovered from scrap and extensively repaired. Baldwin 2-8-0 No 18 is a perfect example. In recent years too, Duran has completely removed most of its machinery from old wooden buildings to a more modern workshop; all of this took place whilst regular maintenance was also taking place. This activity serves to verify in no uncertain way, that the finest investment the ENFE has is in its staff. It seems to be the lot of anyone who works on railways, sometimes to be in the midst of the most abject misery and discomfort. And yet, ENFE railway staff always seem to be cheerful, hard-working, and take disasters in their stride. During the unforgettable flooding of 1982, even the office staff at Riobamba took to the pick and shovel to try to clear and recover the mud-filled line, indicating their devotion to duty.

Another important feature of the G&Q is its ferry link. The rail terminal at Duran is situated on the opposite bank of the River Guayas to that of the city. In order to start one's journey from Guayaquil it is first necessary to cross this mile-wide span. The passenger ferry bridges the gap and for about 3p one can enjoy the 10min cruise to Duran. Around 1976 a road bridge, consisting of two huge concrete spans, was constructed further upstream, crossing the River Daule, and River Babahoyo, passing by Duran, but the railway's ferry still has the edge for convenience and cheapness.

In order to bring rail freight across to Duran, a huge steel raft is employed upon which are two railway tracks, with capacity for four bogied wagons. The raft is attached to a tug; at each side of the river a steel pontoon mates with the tracks, allowing the wagons to be rolled on or off.

The road bridge at Duran, and indeed all of the roads developed in Ecuador in recent years, has systematically reduced the importance of Ecuador's railway. In contrast to the limited services of the G&Q, (one mixed train per day plus a number of railbuses), there are now prolific bus services to and from almost every small town. The bus journey between Quito and Guayaquil can be comfortably accomplished in about 6hr. (Again the word 'comfortably' must not be taken literally; the journey by bus is far from comfortable, and relies too much on the passenger's good relationships with the Almighty). Most business people now fly between Guayaquil and Quito, a 30min flight, in contrast to some 15hr by train.

It is laudable that the government of Ecuador continues to run the ENFE. It is operated principally for the less-privileged, fares are incredibly cheap, some 15p for the 90 kilometres from Duran to Bucay for example. The ENFE says that it would not like to increase fares greatly, and feels a social responsibility for the people who depend on the railway. The G&Q is indeed a lifeline for the smaller towns north of Bucay. They more than anyone are feeling the cut in services because they are almost entirely railway-dependent.

Locomotive Stock of the G&Q, 20 January 1988

Steam	Loco No	Status/Location
Baldwin 2-6-0s	7	Stored at Duran
	11	In steam, Duran/Bucay
	14	Under repair, Duran, since July 1987
Baldwin 2-8-0s	(15)	Static museum exhibit at National Unity Street, Riobamba
	17	Under light repair, Duran
	18	Major rebuild (recovered from scrap)
	(38)	Withdrawn at Riobamba, being cannibalised for parts
	43	Under heavy repair, Bucay
	44	Under light repair, Bucay
	45	In steam, Bucay
	46	Serviceable, Bucay
	53	Under boiler repair, Duran
	58	Serviceable, Bucay

Locomotives whose numbers are bracketed are not capable of return to service.

Diesel

Alsthom diesel locomotives, at Ibarra and San Lorenzo. From an original complement of five locomotives, numbered 151-155 Nos 151, 152 and 155 reported serviceable.

Alco Co-Co diesel-electric locomotives. From a complement of 10 locomotives numbered 160-169, Nos 160, 162, 165, 168, 169 and one unidentifiable due to fire, at Quito. Nos 161 and 166 and Bucay under light repair. Two units could not be traced. The number of serviceable units was uncertain, but it was believed that two locomotives could be returned to service.

NB This list is an assessment of the locomotive stock, not an official record.

It is hoped that the civil engineers of the *Ministerio de Obras Publicos* can soon conclude their surveys, and that the detour will soon be constructed. In an election year for the Democratic Republic of Ecuador, it is hoped that the new government will continue to shoulder the responsibility of the ENFE. Hopefully it will not be too long before the cannon fire of the heavy Baldwin 2-8-0s, or indeed the roar of the Alco diesels can be heard again echoing across the Devil's Nose.

To finish this article, I cannot resist recalling a footplate trip made on 2-8-0 No 44 in August 1987. On arrival at the water tower just before Milagro, the crew were obviously concerned that something was amiss. On stopping, it transpired that the left side pony truck axlebox was running hot. The train was backed up a little so that the offending axle was aligned to the water tower delivery pipe, and the water turned on. Unfortunately, although the onlookers became quite soaked, not much of this water was reaching its target, ie the hot axlebox. By now quite a large lake was forming around the locomotive; the crew took it in turns to wring out soaking cotton waste on to the axlebox, which hissed like spit on an electric iron, until finally it had cooled enough to move on into Milagro. At Milagro, the crew seemed to be gathering some loose change together; one of them ran off to the shops, returning later with some strips of fatty pork meat from a nearby butchers. This meat was ceremoniously tied on to the axlebox. The crew then seemed quite satisfied to continue; if, along our way, we could smell pork cooking, we would know that we had to stop to cool off again! As it happened, the axlebox behaved itself for the rest of the journey. I doubt if the crew would ever know that they were using a technique once used by the LNER on the middle big-ends of Gresley Pacifics, some of which contained a glass vial of strong-smelling chemical. The vial would burst if overheated, the smell would warn the crew to take action. The crew of No 44 deserve full marks for initiative on this occasion!

I sincerely hope to be able to return to Ecuador in the future, and to be able to travel once more all the way from Duran to Riobamba by rail. Meanwhile I wish the ENFE well in its task ahead, and in particular I must thank Sñr Luis Zapata, Chief Superindendent at Riobamba, and Sñr Carlos Ron, Station Chief at Quito, for taking the time and trouble to provide much of the data for this article, and finally for the assistance of all ENFE staff, fitters and enginemen, whose cheerful co-operation will never be forgotten.

Fig 6

Gradient chart: Guayaquil-Quito-San Lorenzo (Ecuador).

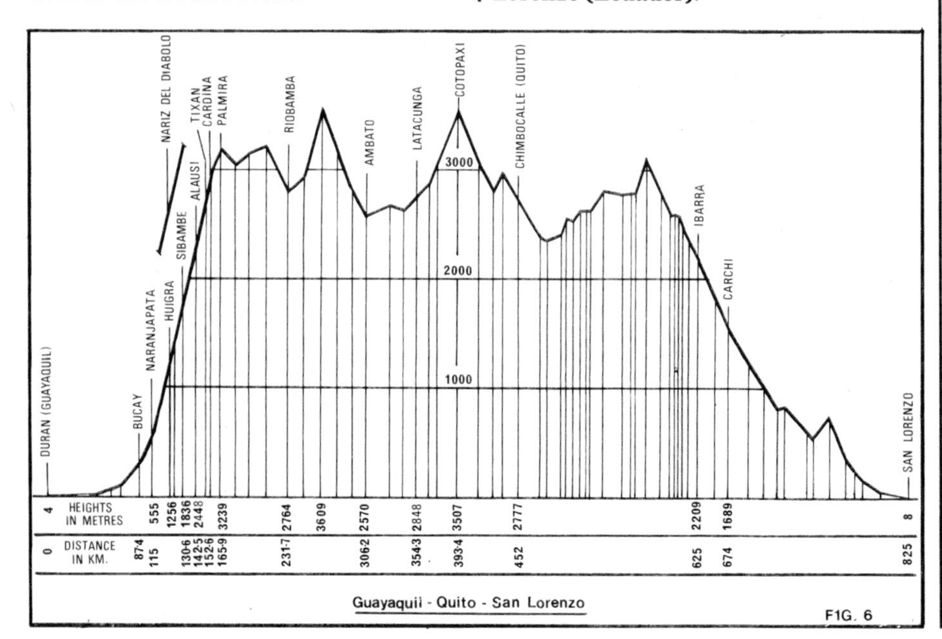

Below:

Autoferro No 04 waits at Yaguachi *en route* for Guayaquil, having just let the 'Mixto' through to Milagro. *Gil Hughes*

At the Time of Going to Press.

British Steam Locomotive Preservation Update

Above:
By any standards, the resurrection of BR '8' Pacific No 71000 *Duke of Gloucester* is an extraordinary achievement, particularly if it returns to main line service. At Didcot, 16 July 1988. *John B. Gosling*

Michael Harris

The pages of the railway enthusiast press, if examined over a decade, would run *Old Codger's Almanac* a close second in terms of confident and unrealised predictions. On numerous occasions, the fateful words 'at the time of going to press No 1234 is expected to be back in steam this summer . . .' have proved to be, ahem, somewhat optimistic. Indeed, there are several locomotives whose resurrection has been greatly exaggerated, to misuse a well-known quotation. Before looking at what is going on in the British locomotive preservation 'industry' it is worth considering some of the realities of the process.

In steam days, locomotives went to main works for several classifications of overhaul or repair. Main works general overhauls were something not undertaken lightly and occurred at, say, 100,000-mile intervals. During their lives, locomotives were not merely repaired but frequently whole units were replaced or renewed. The Gresley 'A3' Pacifics, for instance, often had three-quarters of their main frames replaced by new, while new boilers and cylinders might be fitted two, three or four times during the life of a locomotive. Consequently, of, say, *King George V* or *Flying Scotsman* very little remains of the locomotive 'as built' other than the driving wheel centres and nameplates. Possibly some of these renewals were uneconomic by today's standards but, when materials and labour were comparatively cheap, the principle was, when in doubt, renew. Such opportunities are not open to today's locomotive owners who have had to explore all means of repairing existing components as in many cases the technology no longer exists to manufacture new items. However, over the 30 years of locomotive preservation to date, the capabilities of restoration groups and preserved railway workshops have steadily developed. In the early days of British preservation, locomotives were acquired from BR on the basis of their general good condition. Then came the Barry phenomenon and locomotives were purchased by groups in a variety of conditions. Their owners have had to develop a range of abilities to cope with cracked frames, doubtful boilers and wasted platework.

A recent Great Western Society

44871
44871

newsletter outlined the 'can do' philosophy well. 'In the early days of preservation, anything beyond retubing a boiler was almost beyond contemplation and it was something of a milestone when, 15 years ago, the GWS was the first to lift the boiler of a main line locomotive . . . nowadays we would not bat an eyelid at the prospect! [Retyring of locomotive wheelsets] was something deemed impossible in the early years . . . now there are currently four locomotives at Didcot for which new driving wheel tyres have been manufactured . . .'

So the 'state of the art' has progressed mightily, but there are certain insuperable problems in the business of overhaul, well appreciated by anyone contemplating household DIY. Until you have stripped down the object of attention, you cannot properly assess what needs to be renovated. The first job on undertaking an overhaul is to reduce the locomotive to a kit of parts . . . and that is when the problems start. Whether the locomotive has been in traffic, or has arrived from Barry, the likelihood is that more items for attention will be revealed once it is possible to examine components from all angles. In steam days, defective items would be discarded very often, to be replaced by new or exchange items on hand. Nowadays, it is a question of remanufacture or careful repair, by building up wasted items by welding or by using metal spraying or stitching techniques. Fortunately, several preservation or specialist workshops can cast and machine replacement components, but it all takes time. Also, specialist boiler repair facilities are relatively few and far between and many locomotive owners have to take their place in a queue. Not least, when so much work is being carried out by volunteers, there are only so many hours in the day to undertake dirty, heavy and tiring tasks. Given that most restoration teams are operating in far from ideal conditions, it is a wonder that so much excellent and competent work is carried out.

With the foregoing in mind, it is not surprising that confident predictions of the return of a locomotive to service are often over-optimistic. Very often, the commercial people involved with a preserved railway, or the owners of locomotives passed for running on the main line, are anxious for an engine to return to steam in order to generate revenue. So their eagerness in setting deadlines can be appreciated. British locomotive operators should congratulate themselves on the generally high standard of work achieved. Frequently, BR mechanical inspectors are called in for

Left:
LMS '5' 4-6-0 No 44871 (nowadays named *Sovereign*) is back on the main line. It is seen here at Steamtown, Carnforth nearing the end of its overhaul, in summer 1988. *S. W. Atherton*

Below left:
The Middleton Railway's Sentinel, BR No Departmental 54, is put through its paces shunting at Grosmont while on the North York Moors Railway, 9 October 1988. This engine had been returned to steam after a 12-year absence. *M. Hall*

Below:
'Manor' 4-6-0 No 7828 *Odney Manor* gleams in the sunlight at Bronwydd Arms, Gwili Railway on 21 May 1988. *Bernard McCall*

Above:
The boiler of Stanier Mogul No 2968 had successfully passed its steam test and been reunited with the frames when this sole survivor of its class was photographed at Bridgnorth Locomotive Works on 13 November 1988. *R. Greaves*

advice or to pass repair work done, and often have commented 'I've seen as good in steam days, but none better'.

During 1988, several locomotives made their debut after major overhauls. As far as entry into main line service, these comprised Birmingham Railway Museum's 'Castle' No 5080 *Defiant* and Butterley-based LMS '8F' 2-8-0 No 48151. The latter had been first steamed in June 1987. Both were acquired in scrapyard state from Barry and have performed capably on main line charter trains. No 48151 did particularly well, not only on LSW 150 specials to and from Salisbury, but also over the Settle & Carlisle line. Dinting's double-chimney 'Jubilee' No 45596 *Bahamas* was purchased direct from BR but after a very few main line trips in the early 1970s was out of traffic until the completion of its overhaul in September 1988. Proudly wearing its BR green livery, the 'Jubilee' should return to main line metals during 1989. Less expected on the national 'territory' was the *Port Line* Locomotive Project's 'Merchant Navy' No 35027 *Port Line*. This attracted admiring glances from visitors to the Woking 150 event in May 1988, and then went on to haul passenger services for the Bluebell Railway during the summer. This was the 142nd locomotive to leave Barry scrapyard (in December 1982) and its owners have done a fine job to return it to service so quickly. In fact, it is the most recent Barry departure to have been steamed. No 35027 was largely restored by the group at the Swindon Heritage Centre where the members are now energetically tackling unrebuilt 'Battle of Britain' Pacific No 34072 *257 Squadron*.

Other ex-Barry locomotives back at work have included 'Manors' No 7822 *Foxcote Manor* on the Llangollen Railway (first steamed in 1987) and No 7828 *Odney Manor*, on loan to the Gwili Railway during the summer of 1988. Expected as an imminent main line performer is rebuilt 'West Country' No 34027 *Taw Valley*, based on the Severn Valley Railway, which saw some running to and from Bridgnorth during 1988. Although it is difficult to include exhaustive coverage within the limits of a short article, other notable performers in 1988/89 included the Middleton Railway's Sentinel four-wheeler No 54, back at work for the first time since 1976, and the appearance on the Ffestiniog Railway of Hunslet 2-6-2T *Russell*. This engine was back in traffic on its home Welsh Highland Railway in 1987 but, resplendent in gleaming paintwork, made the journey across to Porthmadog Harbour for limited workings over the FR during the Steam 125 celebrations in April 1988. This engine represents one of the longest and most patient restoration projects, having last steamed in the early 1950s, and was then in the process of resurrection from the early 1960s.

Looking to the locomotives that doubtless will be attracting the photographers at the time *Railway World Year Book* is published, two stalwart main line performers in recent years should head the list: LMS '5' No 44871 (nowadays named *Sovereign* after a RN fleet submarine) and 'King Arthur' No 777 *Sir Lamiel*. No 44871 was one of the four engines for BR's Last Steam Train in 1968, and although based at Steamtown, Carnforth has been jointly overhauled there and in Scotland. Appropriately, No 44871 should be at work north of the Border for the Fort William-Mallaig steam service, along with sister '5' No 5305. No 44871 has been absent from the main line for 11 years. *Sir Lamiel* has proved to be one of the star successes of the Return to Steam, this National Collection engine having been expertly restored by the Humberside Locomotive Preservation Group. From 1982-87, No 777 put up some splendid main line running, particularly out of Marylebone on 450-500-ton 'Shakespeare Limiteds' when its performances often would not have disgraced a Class 8 Pacific. The HLPG has negotiated a further seven-year lease on the locomotive from the National Railway Museum and, during 1988/89, it was extensively overhauled by the HLPG at Hull, funded entirely by the Group. This work has included extensive frame repairs ('Arthurs' were prone to frame fractures and No 777 was no exception), boiler retubing, full motion overhaul and firebox stay renewal — and much else. This should see Maunsell's doughty 4-6-0 back at work on the main line until 1996, naturally assuming BR allows steam to continue.

Other main line performers into the 1990s which should make their debut in the coming year include the unique BR '8' Pacific No 71000 *Duke of Gloucester* which received (almost) all new tyres at Crewe Works in 1987 and recently has had work carried out on the boiler at Didcot Railway Centre in order for it to comply with BR main line running requirements. Another Class 8 locomotive confidently expected to make its debut on the main line is 'King' No 6024 *King Edward I*. Since 1973 members of its owning Society have laboured mightily at Quainton Road on the restoration of the 'King', with much work initially carried out on a siding in all weathers. Steaming was expected to have taken place in the spring of 1989, the engine later moving to a steam centre with a main line connection so that further work could be undertaken in order to prepare No 6024 for its main line certificate.

Two other Class 8 locomotives are also undergoing major overhauls for return to the main line: 'Duchess' No 46229 *Duchess of Hamilton* and — a longer term prospect — 'Princess' No 6203 *Princess Margaret Rose*. Both these engines had been owned by Butlins and have now been purchased, by the NRM and Midland Railway Trust respectively. No 46229 should regain BR metals in 1989 after a four-year overhaul in which the major replacement of platework, particularly on the tender, has necessarily taken longer than was first estimated.

One feature of today's preservation scene is the considerable work now undertaken at the major steam centres where progress is often in hand on several locomotives at the same time, usually involving the owning groups working with the centre's locomotive engineering team. Bridgnorth, on the Severn Valley Railway, probably heads the list in terms of engines 'on works'. Here a rebuilt locomotive works is taking shape in order to provide greatly improved working facilities, at the same time making it a better neighbour for local residents. Before building work begins in earnest, several restoration projects that have been in hand for some time must be completed. In particular, there is the interest of seeing three Moguls being outshopped for service: LNER 'K4' 2-6-0 No 3442 *The Great Marquess*, scheduled for outshopping in spring 1989 after a lengthy sojourn at Bridgnorth; GWR '43XX' No 9303 and LMS 2-6-0 No 42968. The last had its final steam test in October 1988, after which reassembly took place. It had been hoped that No 42968 would have been back in service by 1987, but its owners, the Stanier Mogul Fund — like so many restoration teams — have been faced with engineering tasks that have exceeded the time limit because additional renewals have been necessary and, consequently, the original budget for overhaul has over-run. No 42968 is expected to be ready for revenue earning service at the start of the 1990 season, over 16 years since it left Barry and 23 years or so since it was withdrawn by BR.

The Erlestoke Manor Fund's work on the restoration of 'Manor' No 7802 *Bradley Manor* has been regularly reported in *Railway World* during the last few years. This engine, once used for Royal Train haulage, was originally purchased as a source of spares but the decision was then taken to restore No 7802 in its own right. This engine, too, is a candidate for return to service in the next year.

The Sheffield Park Works of the Bluebell Railway is another hive of activity and here three more ex-Barry locomotives are making good progress towards steaming: 'S15' 4-6-0 No 847 (awaiting a number of fitting out jobs), '9F' 2-10-0 No 92240 (whose boiler passed its hydraulic test in 1988) and BR '5' 4-6-0 No 73082 *Camelot* which is being reassembled.

One Bluebell locomotive has been away from home for four years, 'Dukedog' 4-4-0 No 3217 *Duke of Berkeley*. Work has been in hand on No 3217 at the Didcot Railway Centre, including new tyres fitted to the driving wheels. Returned to the Bluebell early in 1989, further work is envisaged before its reappearance in traffic. Didcot's new Locomotive Works and Lifting Shop is now in the last stages of the overhaul of No 5029 *Nunney Castle* which is expected to be be in operation alongside sister engine *Drysllwyn Castle* during the 1989 season, before the latter is withdrawn for boiler repairs. Somewhat smaller in size, and now being reassembled although a new boiler is required, is 0-4-0ST No 1340 *Trojan*, a GWR 'absorbed' locomotive from the Alexandra Docks & Railway Co. It is significantly one of the few British preserved locomotives to require a replacement boiler, the existing one being beyond economic repair.

At the Buckfastleigh Works of the Dart Valley Railway, the long expected resurrection of 'Hall' 4-6-0 No 4920 *Dumbleton Hall* is now imminent, after a restoration task that has been protracted by the unwelcome discovery of items that needed further attention. Previous expected returns to service were for 1985, then 1987. By October 1988, the boiler was again reunited with

Below left:
Last stages — preparations are made to refit the smoke deflectors on rebuilt 'West Country' 4-6-2 No 34027 *Taw Valley* at Bridgnorth Locomotive Works on 26 September 1987. *John Bird*

Below right:
Yet another locomotive from Barry scrapyard proudly restored to former glory, as represented by Birmingham Railway Museum's 'Castle' 4-6-0 No 5080 *Defiant* on 18 August 1987, at Tyseley. *John B. Gosling*

the frames, and had previously undergone a static steam test. With good luck, No 4920 should be back in operation by the time the *Year Book* is on sale. This engine is owned by the Dumbleton Hall Preservation Society, but also taking shape (literally) at Buckfastleigh is the DVR's own 'hybrid' '64XX' 0-6-0PT. This comprises the frames of No 6435, the wheels and boiler from No 6430 and the remaining superstructure of No 6435. The finished result will be — No 6435!

Farther north, one likely candidate for rebirth in the near future is '45XX' 2-6-2T No 4561 being restored with gusto on the West Somerset Railway. The boiler was repaired by the Severn Valley Railway and successfully test steamed late in 1988. Now work proceeds on the frames, with a more than usually confident forecast of a return to service of the Prairie in late 1989.

At the North Staffordshire Railway Co's Cheddleton centre, it is hoped that LMS '4F' 0-6-0 No 4422 will be steamed in 1989 after a painstaking restoration.

So far we have been concerned with locomotive restoration progress in England. This is not to say that locomotive engineers have been resting on their laurels in the rest of the British Isles, but merely reflects the concentration of railways and steam in England.

One locomotive that has been the subject of continual enquiries as to when — or if — it would be restored, is the Barclay 0-4-2WT No 7 of the Talyllyn Railway. Befitting its original owners — Bord na Mona (the Irish Turf Board) — this engine is known as *Irish Pete*, an example of a rare play on words in the fairly unjokey railway preservation movement. Now, however, *Irish Pete*, after years of storage at the TR's Pendre Works, is undergoing overhaul although its reappearance in steam is so far *sine die*. The reason is one both familiar and frequent. Workshop space, and the availability of labour and finance, are necessarily devoted to maintaining existing serviceable locomotives. Railways and steam centres obviously have to concentrate their resources on turning out locomotives each season to operate their booked duties. Major restoration projects have to take their turn behind more immediately available motive power, hence *Irish Pete's* long period of inactivity.

Above:
Hunslet 2-6-2T *Russell* represents a remarkable exercise in persistence in the return of a once worn-out locomotive to pristine condition. The locomotive is seen at the Welsh Highland Railway's shed, 26 August 1988. *C. A. Klein*

Much farther north, the Strathspey Railway is home to Caledonian 0-6-0 No 828, for some time a static exhibit at the original location of the Glasgow Museum of Transport. However, No 828 has been on the Strathspey since 1980, with the aim of returning the 0-6-0 to service. After overhaul elsewhere of the boiler, work is now in hand on the engine's reassembly.

Across the Irish Sea, the fine work of the Railway Preservation Society of Ireland is an inspiration to the whole railway movement. Again, the main concentration has been on maintaining the Society's splendid tally of locomotives for regular operations over the Irish railway network. But one interesting locomotive is progressing steadily towards its debut in service. This is Dublin & South Eastern Railway 2-6-0 No 15, CIE No 461, an inside cylinder design. The 2-6-0 was received on permanent loan from CIE in 1977, and arrived at the Whitehead base of the RPSI in 1984. Since then, work has steadily proceeded with its overhaul, made difficult by the absence of several components and damage to others, including the cutting through of the right-hand piston rod. Much platework was rotten, particularly on the tender.

The 'water cart' of many engines has proved to be a major item for attention, as years of inactivity and the residue of rusty water and damp coaldust continue to work their worst. Consequently, what is an often ignored adjunct of an engine absorbs more activity on the part of restorers than is often recognised by the enthusiast. However, No 15/461 is making its way towards completion which should come in the next year or so.

Having made our way around necessarily only a selection of railways and steam centres, the reader will see that, all being well, a number of interesting locomotives are near to turning their wheels once more after enforced absences from steaming of anything up to 25 years. Some are already well-known performers from earlier days of preservation, others are unknown quantities at the head of a train. The total sum of work done by an invisible army of locomotive preservation men (and women) is truly staggering and it only remains to say that we are all in their debt. So, the next time you are inclined to be impatient when a favourite engine overruns a deadline that 'by the time this is in print, No 1234 will be back in service', spare a thought for the tribulations of the 'heavy metal' brigade. Better still, drop a few coins into the collecting box on the side of the nearest engine patiently awaiting its return to steam. That way, you will be contributing instead of complaining.

High Speed Train through the Severn Tunnel

Robin Russell

Even when compared with the present day rail tunnelling work of the Europeans and Japanese, the Severn Tunnel is seen as a considerable achievement. Opened just over a hundred years ago, its completion at that time was little short of miraculous.

During the mid-19th century, there was growing concern over the need for trains between London and South Wales to detour via Gloucester. Freight traffic — largely coal — was the predominant problem, and initially a bridge was regarded as the best solution. Sir John Fowler prepared such a scheme in 1865, but Charles Richardson convinced the GWR Board — chaired by Sir Daniel Gooch — that a tunnel was the answer. Parliamentary approval was obtained in 1872, with work commencing the following year.

Test shafts were sunk near the western bank of the Severn (2¼ miles wide at this point) at the village of Portskewett, an office and some workers' cottages having just been completed. The small team of GWR employees, with Sir John Hawkshaw as consultant, made little progress and in August 1877 the directors decided to invite tenders from outside. Two small contracts were let, supplementing the continuing GWR work. By October 1879, only 130yd separated the two tunnelling teams. However, disaster struck in the form of severe flooding. Although no injuries occurred, the effect upon the project was severe. It is noteworthy that the floods were of fresh (spring) water; it had always been assumed that the threat lay in water from the river breaching the tunnel roof.

Hawkshaw was then given total control of the proceedings, demanding the appointment as contractor of Thomas A. Walker, who had a wealth of tunnelling experience, obtained during the construction of London's underground railways, and who also built the Manchester Ship Canal. His first concern was to ensure adequate flood protection. Two massive steam-driven pumps were already on order; the cuttings at each tunnel end were to be protected from high tides by embankments: even at that stage,

Below:

An early view of the east end of the Severn Tunnel, showing the trap to prevent runaway vehicles entering the tunnel. This was later removed. The east end façade is by far the grander of the two. *Locomotive Publishing Co*

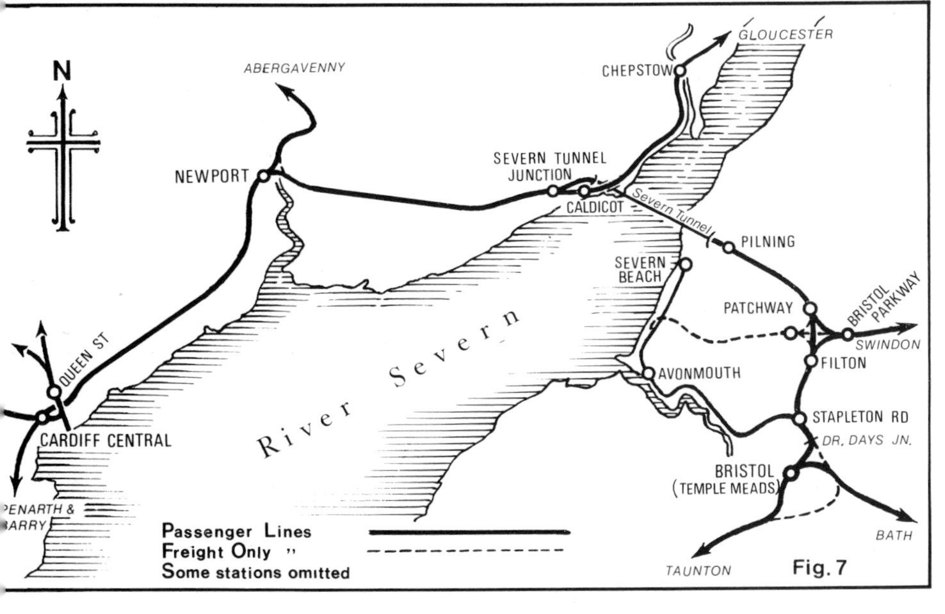

Fig 7
Location of the Severn Tunnel.

river water was still regarded as the greatest hazard and the tunnel line was lowered by 15ft to a total depth of 140ft below rail level on dry land. The realignment resulted in a gradient of 1 in 90 to the west and 1 in 100 to the east. Around this time, workers' accommodation was extended and further workshops built, as was a brickworks: this eventually produced 28 million bricks, supplemented by 19 million from nearby Cattybrook and 29 million from elsewhere. However, before these could be used, the pumping out of the workings was necessary. The two large pumps were delivered, together with a total of 13 Cornish boilers. Pumping was preceded by blanking off the area concerned with two oak shields: this had to be done at the depth of 140ft. Poor quality brickwork meant that cementing was needed to obtain a reasonable seal, the underwater team being led by Lambert, a skilled and intrepid diver. Problems with the pump valves hindered progress, but the water level was gradually lowered.

Additional (vertical) shafts were sunk in the spring of 1880, supplemented by headings (horizontal tunnels). During the summer of that year, further pumps were installed; a massive pump failure, leading to a serious hold-up, was caused by faulty rubber bands (a problem having toy connotations, but all too real). New parts were installed by October, and a massive pumping effort was supplemented by further work on watertight doors, to isolate any further ingress of water. The divers encountered appalling conditions. At one stage, a walk of 1,000ft along a submerged heading proved impossible, due to the length of air hose required, and Lambert was provided with a knapsack containing cylinders of compressed air. The floodwater was under control by the end of the year.

As 1881 commenced, additional accommodation — including a mission hall and a school — was under construction. Mid-January brought with it an unexpected danger. Supplies of coal for the pump boilers had always been taken for granted, by courtesy of GWR freight trains. A massive snowstorm prevented these getting through; coal was obtained from every possible local source, and even wood had to be scavenged to keep the boilers alight until coal supplies resumed.

Above:
This view shows the Welsh end of the Severn Tunnel, and the trap points to prevent any runaway vehicles from entering the tunnel. *Locomotive Publishing Co*

Nature having done its worst, the next episode was a strike in May, which was skilfully handled and shortlived. Present day labour representatives might not have liked the duty arranged for several of the workers a short time later. Flooding in the tunnel proved to be of salt water (the only time when this occurred). To ascertain the position of the river leak, a line of men — with linked arms — walked across the riverbed at low tide. As was hoped, the location was discovered when one of the party temporarily disappeared from sight! A load of clay from a schooner filled the hole, and cement work underneath completed the repair. Later in 1881 electric lighting was installed underground and, for ventilation, both a compressed air main and large fans were provided. Around the same time, the GWR introduced its rock drill, which was stated to be excellent in use but of complicated design, arguably a fair description of the four-cylinder locomotives of G. J. Churchward, who early in his career worked on the layout of the Severn Tunnel pumps. Stationary engines were installed to pull skips of material out by a wire rope, replacing '. . . stout ponies of 13 to 13½ hands high . . . (which) became most intelligent at their work . . .' Further improvements included the extension of electric lighting and the introduction of an underground telephone. These took place in 1882, a year of progress noted for the construction of a hospital. The mission hall burnt down and was completely rebuilt in three weeks.

So 1882 had been a good year, and although the first part of 1883 was marred by a fatal accident, the work was not delayed. In October, however, Lambert had to be called for once again, following a massive flood of fresh water, compounded by a tidal wave which extinguished the fires in the boilers. This major set-back led to the provision of still more pumps, together with Lancashire boilers. A local epidemic of smallpox caused the construction of an isolation hospital, while tunnelling work was fully resumed. The next year, 1884, proved to be the period of maximum employment, with the workforce totalling approximately 3,600 men. John Price controlled the east bank workers, while in Wales the foreman was Joseph Talbot. In October 1884, the anniversary of the 1883 tidal wave, Gooch and another GWR director fortuitously arrived at the site just as the passage from end to end was completed.

During 1885, progress was rapid; opening out the heading to the full-size tunnel was performed in several sections. By April, the brickwork was completed. In September, with water pressure below the tunnel at 45½lb/sq in, the inaugural train passed through, with

Gooch on board. By December, pressure had risen to 57¼lb/sq in so additional pumping capacity was arranged. To the present time, up to 20 million gallons of water are pumped out per day. Currently, the air is changed at a rate of 800,000sq ft/min.

Freight traffic through the tunnel commenced in September 1886, with passenger trains operating from the following July. Aside from the references to Lambert, little mention has been made of the conditions under which the tunnellers worked. These — and all other aspects of the entire, fascinating, project — can be studied in detail by reference to the Kingsmead Reprints edition of Walker's *The Severn Tunnel, its construction and difficulties.* A chapter in Beaver's *A History of Tunnels*, published by Davies, provides a good summary.

Moving on to recent times, I had the most interesting experience of travelling the Severn Tunnel route at the front end of a Western Region IC125 unit train, the cab pass being provided by Ian Body and Christian Tagholm at 125 House, Swindon. With memories of Severn Tunnel expresses of the past — 'Irish Mail', 'Red Dragon', 'Capitals United', 'Pembroke Coast Express' — I proceeded to Paddington on the morning of 3 May 1984. Whatever one thought about GWR locomotive practice and performance, Paddington — which was originally to have been built in the Euston area — is superb. The *Illustrated London News* in 1854 described it as '. . . erected . . . in accordance with the magnificent railway itself'. Michael Harris, writing in the 1980 *Railway World Annual*, refers to a '. . . noble station . . . not spoilt by change . . .' So, among the ghosts of 'Castles' and 'Kings', I found — already standing at Platform 6 — the Cardiff express 1C20.

The train had already worked up from Swansea that morning, with Drivers Graham Jones and Ken Roberts, to whom I was introduced by Chief Regional Traction Inspector John Barrett. I was given some basic information concerning the powercar, No 43014. It was constructed in four sections: cab, clean air compartment (electrical and brake equipment), engine compartment and guard's van. Two four-wheeled bogies are driven on all axles. Car weight is 66 tons, and tractive effort is 17,980lb. The Valenta engine is a development of the earlier Ventura.

We soon received the signal to start, and left Paddington just after 10.00am. The controller was immediately set at the final — fifth — position, giving an engine speed of 1,500rpm (idling is at 750rpm; the overspeed governor operates at 1,800rpm). Accelerating the train at the full power of the two 2,250hp engines did not activate the wheel slip detectors, nor exceed the speed limits. For approximately half a mile, the restriction is 25mph, progressively rising through 60mph and 85mph to 125mph. Five minutes after departure we were up to 97mph at Acton, soon afterwards racing past the Underground trains at Ealing Broadway. The controller was eased back to position three as we reached 125mph just before West Drayton. Passing Slough I recalled that Queen Victoria, *en route* to Windsor Castle, frequented this station which was opened in 1838, one year after her coronation.

We slowed to 100mph for the bridge over the Thames, just before Maidenhead, and I noted the operation of the cab equipment. The AWS bell rang at every green signal, other aspects operating a buzzer and applying the brakes within 3sec unless the warning is cancelled. Once a minute the vigilance buzzer sounded; again, brakes are applied if there is no cancellation. A further aid to safe travel is the facility for installing AWS magnets at the site of pw restrictions. As we entered Sonning cutting, opened in 1840 and originally planned to be a tunnel, power was eased off for Reading, where the Taunton route bears left and I was shown the yellow HST warning lines on the platforms. I had my first view of a Class 58 3,300hp freight locomotive as we left the station.

Shortly after Goring, previously the site of the much-photographed water troughs, I was discussing with John Barrett the remarkable quiteness and smoothness of the ride in the air-conditioned cab. He explained that suspension is primarily on coil springs, with a secondary flexicoil spring system, both supplemented with hydraulic dampers. Trouble-free running of all HST units is aided by a twice daily A exam, a weekly B exam and a C exam once a month. A day's running can total 1,000 miles, but this is well within the range of the fuel supply. I was told that our track consisted of 113lb/yd rail, with 28 concrete sleepers per 60ft track length, and 15in of granite ballast below the sleepers.

The quadruple track section from Paddington came to an end as we approached Didcot (one of the stations offering the excellent scheme of free parking for passengers), junction for Oxford. To the west, signalling is installed (albeit at wider intervals) for reverse-flow traffic on the lines to Chipping Sodbury (on our route) and Thingley Junction (on the Bath line). This

Below:
On the author's trip an eastbound IC125 set is passed near Bristol Parkway.
Robin Russell

Getting nearer to the Severn the traveller glimpses this unusual view of the up portal of Cattybrook Tunnel. *Robin Russell*

is used for emergencies and engineering work, but not for peak one-way traffic diversions; crossovers are provided approximately every 10 miles. Other features of the Western Region main line include hotbox detectors every 25 miles or so, and junctions aligned to diverge at 70mph, which are signalled by a flashing yellow aspect (for a lower-speed turnout, the signal does not clear until the train has almost stopped). Recent innovations include sirens on certain limited visibility curves to warn pw workers of approaching trains, and safety fences every 50yd where trackside clearance is limited. Safety requirements extend to the IC125 unit's braking system; disc brakes are used throughout, supplemented by tread brakes on the power cars.

A brake application was made as we sighted a yellow aspect which cleared to green shortly afterwards, just before the pair of level crossings at Steventon and Causeway. As we passed Wantage Road there were memories of the 1857 0-4-0WT *Shannon* which was for many years displayed on the platform of the erstwhile station. Next came Swindon, steeped in GWR history and the same height above sea level as the top of St Paul's Cathedral, followed by Wootton Bassett, where we diverged at 70mph from the line to Thingley Junction and Bath. Rapid acceleration downhill was followed by the 1 in 300 climb past the speed restricted tunnel at Alderton, where the absence of ventilating shafts causes high air pressure. Over the summit, we passed Badminton, precisely 100 miles from London, at 116mph in 58min from the start. A long run downhill at 1 in 300 took us through Chipping Sodbury Tunnel and past Westerleigh Junction, where the line to Gloucester heads north.

Bristol Parkway is at the end of the IC125 line, so we settled down to 90mph travel as we neared the western extremity of the 1903 cut-off from Wootton Bassett to Patchway. From here, up and down lines take separate tunnels at Cattybrook; eastbound steam trains faced slippery rails and dense smoke through the 1 in 100 single bore. Soon after Cattybrook brickworks, we passed Pilning. This was a remarkable location in the days of steam; not only the eastern terminus for the Severn Tunnel car service, but also a favourite location for shots of 28XX-hauled coal trains. I visited the station shortly after my 1984 trip: it was fascinating to see the IC125s flash past the site of my 1950s steam train photographs.

Down through the long approach cutting, and we had entered the Severn Tunnel. Travelling at 70mph we took under 4min to pass through and my thoughts dwelt — by no means for the last time — on the men who toiled in that wet and hazardous environment a century ago. Out into daylight, we climbed to Severn Tunnel Junction, suffering a signal check. Soon after — away on the left — is the Llanwern Steelworks, which uses some of the spring water pumped from the tunnel. We ran slowly into Newport, where we saw a pw train of 60ft track sections. Restarting, we took the crossover at 20mph and entered Hillfield Tunnel on the short run to Cardiff. On the approach we were a little early and were checked,

Right:
This recent cab view of the climb out of the Severn Tunnel on the Welsh side shows no trap points, following the elimination of unfitted freight working on the main line. *Robin Russell*

Left:
A Cardiff-bound IC125 unit enters the east end of the tunnel. *Robin Russell*

obtaining the two white light signal permitting drawing ahead towards an occupied platform. We came to a stand at 11.42½, half a minute early after a remarkable journey which included the 4 mile 628yd tunnel.

I returned through the tunnel as an IC125 passenger a couple of hours later. It was a most enjoyable journey, complemented by an excellent meal. In fact, just as an exercise, I endeavoured to fault the restaurant car: the only possible criticism was that some of the fluorescent lights had been replaced by tubes of a slightly different colour! My thoughts moved on to the competing modes of transport. Air travel is expensive and journeys to and from airports are often time consuming. One does not arrive fresh and fed after road travel, especially by coach, while car parking can be difficult at urban destinations. Rail travel has certainly improved vastly since the opening of the Severn Tunnel and the InterCity trains provide a high level of speed, comfort and convenience.

Right:
A westbound IC125 set screams up the grade from the Severn Tunnel heading towards Cardiff. *Robin Russell*

Bottom:
After arrival at Cardiff Central on the author's westbound journey, the cab crew and inspector pose alongside powercar No 43014. *Robin Russell*

"THEY SAID THERE WAS A SPARE 'THIRTY SEVEN' AT DIDCOT, SO WE TOOK IT!"

Top:
Beyer Peacock 0-6-4T *Lough Melvin* is prepared at Enniskillen for a trip with the 2pm goods to Sligo over the Sligo, Leitrim & Northern Counties Railway, in September 1957. *Robin Stieber*

Mixed feelings:

A Journey on the Sligo, Leitrim & Northern Counties Railway

Robin Stieber

The trouble with visits to railways of character is that so often nothing really happens. The enthusiast boards a train at one end of the line and leaves it at the other, having made notes of locomotives, rolling stock and other items of historical importance; but the journey itself is normal, efficient and relatively dull. From the railway's point of view of course this is as it should be, but for the traveller there is nothing to mark his visit as something special, nothing to set it apart in his mind from the scores of similar visits he may have made to any branch lines anywhere.

It was my good fortune that my last visit to the Sligo, Leitrim & Northern Counties Railway (SL&NCR) should have culminated in a journey which was worth any amount of stocklists and working timetables. The SL&NCR in any case was an individualistic line in most respects. The last privately-owned railway in Ireland, thanks to the border, with its switchback route and hire-purchase locomotives, was naturally in a class of its own. In September 1957 the news from Ireland suggested that a large part of the Great Northern Railway (GNR) and its associated lines, including the SL&NCR, would not survive the month. In company with a friend, and, it seemed, half the railway enthusiasts of England, I went to pay my last respects.

We had planned a timetable which allowed us to sample the line and its motive power very fully. First we travelled on the 7.20pm mixed train from Enniskillen, for many years the only steam-hauled passenger train on the line. The next morning we returned from Sligo on the 9.30am railbus, and finally permission was obtained to ride on the footplate and in the guard's van of the 2pm freight from Enniskillen. As it was all part of a wider tour including the County Donegal Railway and the Cavan & Leitrim, bad timekeeping would have inconvenienced us considerably, but I was confident that since dieselisation of the West Clare, Ireland was a country in which one could travel with at least some hope of an eventual arrival.

The first two parts of the journey were uneventful and prompt. I rode on *Lough Erne*, one of the postwar Beyer Peacock 0-6-4Ts, as far as

Fig 8
The route of the Sligo, Leitrim & Northern Counties Railway, Ireland.

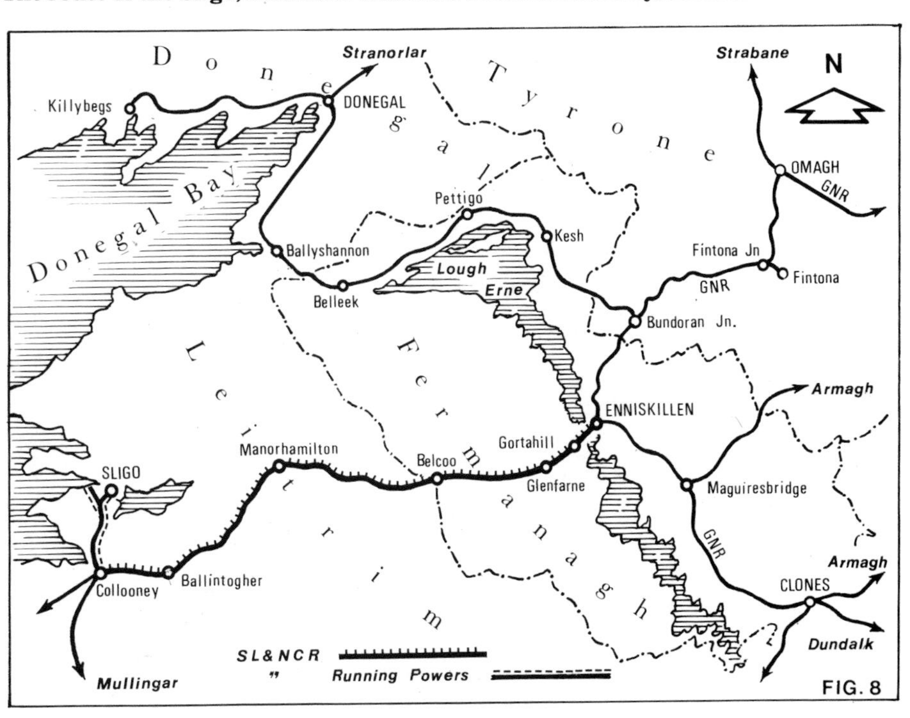

Above:
SL&NCR railcar B, a 5ft 3in gauge articulated railcar by Walker Bros of Wigan, approaches Enniskillen in 1956. The Sligo line curves away in the left background. The foreground tracks are Great Northern. *Colin Boocock*

Manorhamilton on the 7.20pm mixed, continuing to Sligo in the train. On the return trip the next morning we had reason to thank the threatened closure, for under normal circumstances the summer service would have finished 11 days previously, and with it would have gone the 9.30am railbus, leaving us no eastbound train between 6.20am and 4pm. Two years previously I had been obliged to catch the 6.20; a puzzled landlady had left out a flask of coffee for my 5.30am breakfast, and I had groped my way to the station through the dark, deserted streets of Sligo. It was an experience I would not willingly repeat. This year it was broad daylight as Railbus A, its gears grinding hideously, took us back to Enniskillen.

A visit to the GNR shed, lunch, postcards, and two hours later we were once more at the station, watching the 1.45pm railbus leave for Sligo 10min behind time. The goods sidings were full of odd wagons, scattered haphazardly, but there was nothing which even remotely resembled the 2pm freight. On the advice of the ticket collector we crossed the tracks to a low building in the fork of the GNR and SL&NCR tracks south of the station, which served as the main SL&NCR office.

Here we were met by the lady secretary who counselled patience, as it was likely to be some time before our train was ready, gave us indemnity forms to sign, and introduced us to the guard. A few minutes later another enthusiast came in looking for souvenirs, and the secretary at once produced piles of timetables and ready-packed parcels of tickets. This struck me as particularly odd; she had just assured me with the utmost confidence that although only a fortnight remained before all GNR services were withdrawn from Enniskillen, the SL&NCR would be reprieved for at least another year — and yet she was already disposing of the company's tickets in bulk! Hoping that I might yet have the chance to use a first class weekly excursion to Ballintogher, I bought a packet.

Outside in the yard *Enniskillen* and *Lough Melvin* were pottering amiably about with a few wagons. Having ridden on one of the postwar engines the previous night, we hoped that *Enniskillen* would be in charge of the so-called 2pm freight (it was now 2.25pm), but eventually the string of wagons behind *Lough Melvin* grew into something which resembled a train, and stood facing the right direction, so we strolled across to it. I climbed into the brakevan with the guard while Terry presented his credentials to the vast, rotund, silent man in the cab of *Lough Melvin*. At 2.40pm we were away.

I made some hasty calculations. We wanted to reach Dromod that night on the 7pm Sligo-Dublin, for which we would supposedly wait 1¼hr at Collooney. Some 35min of this now remained. Furthermore we intended to visit the works at Manorhamilton during the hour *Lough Melvin* would spend there shunting. From behind 25 wagons of merchandise, I willed the driver on, and indeed he responded magnificently. I may have thought *Lough Erne* a rough rider, but it had been luxury compared with the far end of this loose-coupled freight as we streaked through Florencecourt at fully 35mph, particularly when a bump caught me unawares in the middle of the guard's explanation of the complicated cross-border freight bills, sheets and invoices. At 3.10pm we reached Belcoo, where HM Customs Officer's expression at seeing my by now familiar beard suggested he suspected a smuggling ring at work. Settling his fears, I accompanied him on an inspection of the wagon seals and learned of another mishap to our timetable.

We were supposed to cross the 11am freight from Sligo at Glenfarne, the next station, and exchange crews with it there, but after our 10min shunting at Belcoo, to have gone on would have meant delaying the 11am. Unfortunately this train included a special consignment of cattle from the County Leitrim Fair at Manorhamilton to Enniskillen market and was not to be delayed: so we were held at Belcoo until it arrived.

We leaned on the level crossing gates and muttered about the vagaries of single line working, but the atmosphere at Belcoo was too peaceful for a bad mood to last for long. It was a cool, cloudy aftrnoon. The nearby village was quiet, and the children had come to the station to play. The more intrepid ones were climbing into *Lough Melvin's* cab where a surprise awaited them. Our driver, huge and impressive as ever, was leaning on the side, and as each face appeared in the doorway he smeared a fat, grimy finger across its forehead. Shrieking, the boys fell off, and came back for more. Occasionally the massive frame shook slightly, and a tiny smile appeared to bubble up on to his face, but only for an instant. For most of the time he might have been a priest at some particularly solemn ceremony of anointment.

Nowhere was there any sign of impatience. *Lough Melvin* sat and simmered, the children fought sporadically, we and the staff drowsily waited. An Irish fatalism had settled across the station. At last bells rang, the crossing gates opened, and *Lough Erne* rumbled into Northern Ireland at 4.10pm with its precious load of beef, the mainstay of the SL&NCR. Our siesta was over.

The crews exchanged trains, and we moved off westwards, resuming our previously brisk pace. Skirting the southern edge of Lough Macnean, we soon reached Glenfarne's single platform. They were telephoning Manorhamilton when we arrived. The guard disappeared into the office and came out a minute later. 'They're sending on the four o'clock railbus from Sligo,' he announced, apparently unperturbed. 'We'll cross it here instead of Manorhamilton.' 'And how long will that be?' I asked apprehensively. 'Oh, at least three quarters of an hour.' There was nothing we could do about it, so we sat down on the platform. Glenfarne was clearly a more sophisticated place than Belcoo, for instead of children from the village coming to watch the trains, some girls soon arrived, and under the circumstances the time passed quickly until Railcar B rattled in at 5.20pm. A moment's stop, then it was away, and we were left with a blessedly clear road ahead to Manorhamilton.

From Glenfarne, the line climbs steadily for 4¾ miles to Kilmakerrill Summit. It would have been pleasant to record that *Lough Melvin* did likewise, but I must have walked under a ladder that morning. The first 200 yards of those 4¾ miles were covered without incident; then we stopped sharply. Stalled? Surely not with this load. I leaned out of the van and looked up the train. The fireman had climbed down from the footplate and was inspecting the right-hand inside cylinder. He shook his head, turned, and walked back towards us. 'Cylinder head's blown,' he called. 'We'll have to run back to the station.'

Once more we could only sit and mutter. I even vowed never to complain about British Railways again, a vow which I have of necessity since broken. *Lough Melvin* was obviously unfit to proceed. Very gently the train was eased back into a siding, and the engine parked somehow out of the way. Any hope of making our connection at Collooney was gone, as there was no way of leaving Glenfarne now until the 7.20pm from Enniskillen arrived in about 2hr time, so the village would have to entertain us for that period.

We entered the main street in style in the back of the customs officer's car, and from a general store telephoned the hotel in Sligo at which we had stayed the previous night. On learning that the time of our arrival depended on the SL&NCR at its most whimsical, the manager was understandably doubtful, but eventually agreed to keep a room for us.

The diminutive village of Glenfarne, we discovered upon investigation, unaccountably possessed the only dance hall for many miles around, visited by bands of repute, even by English standards. Tonight, however, it was closed, so with no reluctance at all we prepared to while away our time in the nearby pub. Showing the kind of charity usually reserved for victims of a shipwreck or major railway disaster, the landlady started us off with four large rounds of sandwiches for sixpence before we settled down to the Guinness. After a pint or two, we heard heavy boots outside and the engine crew marched into the bar, their labours with *Lough Melvin* having cost them much sweat in exchange for a healthy thirst. 'I'm looking forward to . . . 's face when he finds what we've got waiting for him here,' beamed the driver lifting his first pint.

'Would he be the redhead who was driving the 7.20 last night as well?' I enquired.

'He would that, and he's a temper to match his hair. There'll be some choice language down at the station when he arrives!' We drank to the forthcoming pleasure.

It was by no means what I had expected to be doing at this time, and it was all the more entertaining for that. There was barely room for the four of us in the tiny pub, with its plain wooden bar, few chairs, and bottles stacked high on the shelves. We talked about railways in Britain, politics in Ireland and politics in Britain, football in Ireland and football in England. The Irishmen had heard of the recent cup exploits of our home team, Bournemouth, particularly since two of its heroes were Irish, and the arguments piled as high as the bottles. At about eight o'clock we thought of the 7.20. 'Ah, never mind him,' grinned the fireman, 'he'll not get past anyway.' True as this undoubtedly was, we had no positive desire to be obstructive, and we wanted a bed that night, so after a large one for the road we made our uncertain way back to the station.

The sight which confronted us was all that our driver had forecast. *Lough Erne* was at the platform with the 7.20, and the staff had given our red-headed friend all the details of the extra wagons he would have to take on to Sligo and the shunting he would have to do at Manorhamilton. It soon transpired

Below:
***Lough Erne* struggles to bring the 11am Sligo-Enniskillen goods train into Belcoo in September 1957.** *Robin Stieber*

that his temper had been precariously strained earlier in the evening. Three other figures were standing on the platform, all of the genus British Railway Enthusiast. We knew them all: one was this afternoon's ticket hunter, the other two had travelled with us from Strabane to Donegal the previous day. At Enniskillen, they told us, they had been talking to the driver, and the former had asked if he might ride on the engine. 'Not without a pass,' was the firm reply. 'Here, borrow mine,' one of the others had said, innocently enough. Many drivers might have been willing to take a passenger aboard with someone else's pass, but not this one. Annoyed at their casual disregard of SL&NCR authority, he curtly refused to take any of them and drove off, sizzling slightly. Now, rather than catch any fresh outbursts from him, the five of us climbed into the leading half-compartment to exchange reminiscences and bawdy songs. The crew of the 2pm train relaxed 'on the cushions' in the next compartment.

Collecting the extra train and coupling it to the 7.20 took nearly half an hour but at last we started westward again. We all held our breath, listening to every laborious puff from *Lough Erne* as it clambered up the hill towards Kilmakerrill. It took 20 long minutes, and Heaven knows what it did to the fire, but the locomotive was in better condition than its sister engine, reaching the halt at the summit without further trouble.

Rather unwisely, when we reached Manorhamilton I went forward to reason with the driver on behalf of the unfortunates who wanted a footplate ride. His hair bristled as he snapped at me, 'Let them on the engine? Ah, no, I've had enough of their tricks. There's nobody I'll have up here now except you. At least I know you've a pass.' In the interests of fraternal harmony among enthusiasts I politely declined, and returned to the compartment. Further along the dimly lit platform things were becoming a little more complicated.

The Fair having finished, crowds of trippers, dealers and other celebrants were waiting impatiently on the station to ride home. Their inhibitions long since washed away, some of them had objected loudly to being delayed, and now even more loudly at the news that *Lough Erne* would have to spend the next half hour or so shunting before the train could proceed. Possibly if there had been another locomotive the passenger coaches might have been sent on separately — but *Sir Henry* and *Hazlewood* were in the works, *Lissadell* was derelict, *Lough Gill* at Dundalk, and *Lough Melvin* a cripple at Glenfarne. On hearing harsh words uttered we shut the carriage door and fastened the window. We did not wish to become involved in an Irish fight.

At length, jolting away from Manorhamilton through the night, we came to Collooney where we waited while more interminable shunting took place. A few miles later on, at Ballysodare, the guard came round for our tickets. We allowed him to see them, but insisted on keeping them for souvenirs, and he capitulated.

At 11.30pm we crawled into Sligo. The 7.20pm was 1hr 50min late, the 2pm goods was 4½hr late, and we had taken 8hr 50min to cover the 48¼ miles. 'We could have walked it quicker,' I grumbled as we left the grim Norman fortress of a station along with many disgruntled natives, but I think none of us really minded. It was a journey of which Percy French could have been proud.

Next morning, when I purchased the CIE winter timetable, which had been in use for about a week, I found that the train we had intended to catch at Collooney, the 7pm from Sligo to Dublin, no longer ran. If we had caught the only remaining train to Dromod that evening we would have been stranded there, with no connection up the Cavan & Leitrim to Ballinamore. Dromod is a charming little place in which to pass an hour or so, but its tourist accommodation is decidedly limited. We would have been knocking on cottage doors, or sleeping on the station, neither of them a really satisfactory course for two comfort-loving travellers. Perhaps the leprechauns of the Sligo, Leitrim & Northern Counties Railway were working for us after all!

Above:
Many enthusiasts admired and photographed the ancient 0-6-4T *Lissadell* which stood forlorn and abandoned at Manorhamilton for several years. *Colin Boocock*

Above right:
***Lough Melvin* rests, broken down at Glenfarne, during the episode that is the subject of this article.** *Robin Stieber*

Right:
A year earlier, *Sir Henry* worked the 7.30pm mixed train from Enniskillen to Sligo and was photographed during the customs stop at Belcoo. The leading vehicle is the SL&NCR's bogie tri-composite brake clerestory coach. *Colin Boocock*

Photo Feature:

There are still Trams at Blackpool!

A Blackpool double-deck tram with pole collector trundles along the promenade towards the tower in October 1988. *Colin Boocock*

Colin Boocock

Even though they represent Britain's last tramcars operated on a commercial basis, enthusiasts tend to pass the Blackpool trams by, perhaps oblivious of the fascinating variety of cars which can be seen there. This small selection of photographs was taken one Saturday afternoon in October 1988.

Above:
Double-decker No 712 passes an open top double deck tram near the Savoy Hotel. Both vehicles have pantograph collectors. *Colin Boocock*

Below:
The latest development in Blackpool trams is the small batch of modern chopper-controlled vehicles which normally work on the Fleetwood run. No 644 heads north towards Gynn Square. *Colin Boocock*

Below right:
A more classic design of single deck tram is represented by car No 680, also heading for Fleetwood. *Colin Boocock*

Above:
Blackpool frequently runs one or two old 'preserved' trams in normal service. No 40 is painted as if wood grained, and presents a strikingly Edwardian appearance as it runs from Cleveleys southbound along the promenade bound for the Pleasure Beach.
Colin Boocock

Left:
During the 'season' the Blackpool double-deck trams work the more heavily loaded section between the Pleasure Beach and Bispham or Cleveleys. This one is heading north between the piers in October 1988.
Colin Boocock

Scottish Stations 1923-1988

J. L. Stevenson

In common with the situation on Britain's railways as a whole, there has been a drastic reduction in the number of stations open for business in Scotland. Route mileage north of the border has fallen from a figure of some 3,700 miles in 1923 to the present 1,674 but the number of passenger stations has shown a much steeper decline from 1,167 to 298, the slaughter having taken place mainly between 1950 and 1970. The following table shows the position in terms of the pregrouping operating companies and excludes those stations owned by the North British (40) and Caledonian (3) in England. Stations on joint lines have been included under the company mainly responsible for their design, while stations opened since 1923 and still open have been credited to the company which owned the route in question.

Pregrouping company	*Number of passenger stations 1923*	*1988*	*Percentage still open*
North British	404	111	27%
Caledonian	346	100	28%
Glasgow & South Western	163	36	22%
Great North of Scotland	134	5	4%
Highland	120	46	38%
Total	1,167	298	25%

While it is the custom to brand the Doctor as the arch-fiend behind the elimination of any railway service, it is a fact that well over half of the above station closures occurred before the publication of the Beeching Report in 1963. Indeed, three quarters of the North British station closures had been effected before that momentous date. But the axe certainly fell with a vengeance between 1964 and 1970, since when the situation has been pretty stable, indeed, with the emphasis more on new stations and on reopenings.

The purpose of this review is not to lament the demise of these stations but rather to consider those still open and in particular to indicate where some of the best buildings can yet be found which portray the hallmark of their one-time owning company. The Scottish Region has done much to retain and improve the best of the old buildings where these still have a purpose to serve, but there is a real danger that the characteristics of the five companies' buildings will tend to disappear as changing circumstances, notably destaffing, mean that small structures will suffice. At least it seems that the time has passed when standard bus shelters were the order of the day. There are few sadder sights than that of one of these things where once stood a handsome station building.

The present position can now be considered in relation to each of the Scottish companies.

North British Railway

Great efforts have been made over the past 20 years to brighten up Waverley, starting with the travel centre of 1970, but the station as a whole has few claims to architectural distinction and its east end has become a rather desolate spot with much of its space given up to the Post Office and to staff buildings which may not be to everyone's taste. However, the west end finds great favour with the public and teems with life, also unfortunately with motor vehicles. The honours in Edinburgh are taken rather by Haymarket station which, after surviving many attempts in the 1960s and 1970s to replace it with a hideous office block, has now been splendidly restored and presents at street level a fine appearance.

On the other side of the country Glasgow Queen Street with its graceful arched roof and extended concourse is a pleasure to behold and a remarkable transformation from the smoke-filled horror of earlier days. Great efforts have been made to improve Dundee Tay Bridge station where the street level building is quite attractive. At platform level the scope is limited but the opening out of the approach from the west has made a striking change for the better and bids the passenger to travel forth.

Below:
Glasgow Queen Street is one of BR's most attractive termini. The delicate ironwork of the 1842 roof and arch is clearly seen. *Colin Boocock*

Top:
The graceful exterior of Haymarket station, Edinburgh was cleaned and restored in 1984. It was originally opened in 1842 and served for a time as the headquarters of the Edinburgh & Glasgow Railway. *J. L. Stevenson*

Above:
This October 1988 view of Cupar, opened in 1848 by the Edinburgh & Northern Railway, shows the handsome, symmetrical main building on the northbound platform. There was formerly a middle track through the station. *J. L. Stevenson*

Elsewhere a fair amount of the station style of the North British and its ancestors can still be seen. On the Edinburgh-Glasgow line Croy and the original Edinburgh & Glasgow Railway buildings at Polmont and Linlithgow have been skilfully refurbished, largely retaining their individual styles. Linlithgow in particular deserves study. Both Falkirk stations were in poor condition and new buildings of interesting designs have arisen. East of Edinburgh, Prestonpans, Drem and Dunbar are substantially unchanged, but it is to Fife that the seeker should go to find the best examples of the smaller North British station. Aberdour with its beautiful garden will probably give the greatest pleasure but Kinghorn and Burntisland deserve a visit, the latter with parts of the old building dating from the days before the Forth Bridge. Markinch has a neat building set on a higher level above the platforms but the best two are Ladybank and Cupar. The former still has the junction recalling pre-Tay Bridge days and the latter lies on a sweeping curve. In contrast Leuchars is a comparatively new structure which replaced one burnt by suffragettes in 1913.

In the Glasgow area most of the North British stations are still open but many of the original buildings have been replaced either by prefabricated structures from 1970 onwards or in one or two instances such as High Street by an individual design. However, on one side of both Kilpatrick and Cardross the original buildings remain, dating from the days of the Glasgow, Dumbarton & Helensburgh Railway. Helensburgh Central terminus is much as it was after rebuilding around 1900. A good example of refurbishment is Milngavie which keeps the best features of the original.

Finally, most of the West Highland timber stations with their characteristic design are intact and several are listed buildings which ought to ensure their retention, but the introduction of radio signalling and in most cases the consequent removal of staff must pose a threat. Garelochhead merits particular attention, having been recently carefully restored.

Caledonian Railway

The jewel is Glasgow Central, the concourse of which has undergone much passenger improvement and commercial development. The result in general is very pleasing, much care having been taken to adapt new construction to the superb concept of the original. Viewed from the approaching train, however, the station lacks cohesion and clearly shows that it was built in two stages, the original opened in 1879 and the west side extension dating from the turn of the century.

The massive buildings at Perth have presented problems. Most of the passenger business is now handled on the Dundee platforms at the southeast corner and never comes within the area of the overall roof. This has been considerably cut back but the main structure is more or less intact as are the carriage sidings on the site of the Scottish Central Railway terminus. Aberdeen, although a joint station, was predominantly Caledonian. Its north end has been altered out of all recognition by commercial development but the concourse has been much improved, the façade remains and the south platforms are little changed although the approach lines, laid out on a grand scale, have been drastically simplified in the course of resignalling.

Of the medium-sized stations Stirling is unequalled. Its architecture is first class and the station has benefitted from a new travel centre and associated works. Five miles to the north Dunblane has the same features on a smaller scale but Gleneagles, although substantially unaltered, is now unstaffed and has lost much of its former glory.

Above:
The exterior of Stirling station shows ornamental stonework, crow-step gables and an attractive entrance porch. Seen in October 1988, all are in excellent condition. *J. L. Stevenson*

Wemyss Bay on the Clyde, showpiece of the days of opulence, is still reasonably well tended but illustrates only too well the problems of deciding how best to treat a fine building now far larger than present needs. The electric sets seem to slip in and out almost apologetically! On a more workaday level Gourock has most of its former structure and remains a lively rail-sea exchange point. Greenock Central is now something of a desolate barn, its massive old building too big for today's requirements.

The stations on the Edinburgh-Glasgow via Shotts line are now mostly unstaffed but several retain the main buildings which are of typical Caledonian style. Kirknewton, formerly Midcalder, is the most impressive of these but West Calder, of humbler design, deserves mention and in 1988 was still set off by a lovely garden. On the Carlisle line Lockerbie alone recalls the style once common here with its sandstone buildings and crow-step gables. The bus shelter on the up platform detracts from the scene.

Some of the Cathcart Circle stations have changed little, notably the two-level Pollokshields West and Maxwell Park, but destaffing and the mortality of timber suggests that their days may be numbered. The same applies to Taynuilt on the Oban line on which Dalmally alone seems likely to survive pretty well intact.

Glasgow & South Western Railway

Gone are the magnificent arches of St Enoch, its site now occupied by a modern structure of not dissimilar external dimensions covering a shopping centre. What a pity that in the manner of Manchester Central the shell of the station could not have been adapted.

Of the larger stations Dumfries is the pick. Little altered, the nicely proportioned buildings are excellently tended, but the same sadly cannot be said of nearby Annan, another instance of a substantial building no longer required for railway purposes. Kilmarnock is prominently located above the town but can scarcely be described as beautiful. Almost all its passenger business is now concentrated on the down side which has not greatly changed. Ayr, still dwarfed by the Station Hotel, has lost some of its platform cover but the enclosing of the small concourse in glass provides some compensating comfort. Largs was rebuilt by the LMS in the mid-1930s and has of late been reasonably well refurbished with a reduction in platform faces. Stranraer Harbour station, jutting out into Loch Ryan, is basically unchanged but greatly tidied, having survived several ambitious proposals in the 1970s for complete restoration.

A number of passing stations deserve mention with Troon perhaps as the most pleasant following extensive refurbishment in collaboration with the Railway Heritage Trust in 1986. Irvine and Prestwick were similarly treated and all keep their best features. Saltcoats had had its red sandstone Glasgow-bound building restored and Kilwinning likewise has benefited from collaboration between the Scottish Region and Strathclyde PTE in station improvements associated with electrification. The last named, the junction between the Ayr and Largs lines, has four platform faces, rather a speciality of the G&SW, examples of the same arrangement being at one time found at Annbank, Barassie and Crosshouse. South of Ayr, Maybole's tall building still exists on the now single (former southbound) platform, the late LMS-period Girvan station is in fair shape and Barrhill remains probably as little altered as any. The tiny station and timber signalbox combine with traditional token working to preserve a scene over which time has so far passed lightly.

Finally, mention must be made of one of the joint line stations, Paisley Gilmour Street more G&SW than Caledonian in style. The solidly built and well maintained four-platform station has successfully defied rationalisation. The portion of the building around the entrance at street level, probably the original, is interesting

Great North of Scotland Railway

The almost total eclipse of this company's stations is particularly regrettable as their standard of construction was high and they fitted admirably into their environment. Of the few remaining open the building at Keith (joint GNS and Highland) has been demolished and replaced by a neat new structure while Dyce retains only a small part of the original. However, much of the down side building stands at Inverurie and gives a fair idea of how a fair-sized GNS station looked. On a smaller scale Insch is complete on both sides and it is to be hoped that it will be left thus intact. Huntly is less satisfying, having at one time had an overall roof after the removal of which the remaining impression is something of a makeshift.

A comfort to anyone wishing to study GNS station styles is that many of the buildings both on and off the operational railway are now in private use, an especially good example being Portsoy. Moreover, the impressive GNS Elgin building still exists although largely out of use.

Highland Railway

Not only has the survival rate of Highland stations been higher that that of the other Scottish companies but most of the various styles and periods are still represented. Inverness itself has basically been little altered since early days but much has been done to brighten up its one-time gloomy interior. The recent resignalling has not changed the platform arrangements.

On the Perth line Carrbridge and Aviemore remain very much as they were opened in 1898 while further south all remaining stations have been sympathetically refurbished with the main features retained. Pitlochry has especially pleasing buildings, the main one dating from 1883, but the up side of Dunkeld appears to retain most of the original station of 1856. Blair Atholl main building was curtailed some time ago due to dry rot but the overall scene with the goods and engine sheds still intact is strongly reminiscent of past days.

There have been a score of closures on the North line but few demolitions. Of the 22 stations still open Dingwall is perhaps the most attractive, dating from 1886 and looking particularly well from the spacious forecourt. Fearn is an original Inverness & Ross-shire Railway station as are Tain and Ardgay, each a larger version of Fearn. Further north the style varied as the successive sections of route took shape. Lairg, one of the busier stations is unpretentious but

Top:
The station building at Lockerbie on the West Coast main line has changed little over the years, though the verandah has been reduced. This view is looking north in September 1988. Formerly there was a shed adjoining the main building at the north end, covering the dock used by the Dumfries branch trains. *J. L. Stevenson*

Above:
The verandah of Maxwell Park station on the Cathcart Circle line in Glasgow has surprisingly survived electrification. The unusual design is a feature of the Cathcart Circle stations, but only this one and that at Pollokshields West are on two levels. *J. L. Stevenson*

Golspie has a very handsome building. Wick and Thurso retain their train sheds and have been carefully restored.

The Kyle line stations show much variety and deserve individual study with the exceptions of Stromeferry and Duirnish both reduced to basics, the former having had in the past an overall roof. Kyle of Lochalsh in its superb setting has happily been retained unaltered and Plockton is noteworthy as being the last station to represent the type common on the later branch lines.

Nairn on the East line is excellently maintained and still has its two signalboxes, one at each end of the long crossing loop. Forres sadly is a ghost of its past as a junction and the present building at Elgin dates from the 1970s when it replaced the rather seedy looking Highland station.

The Scottish Region deserves praise for the way in which it is tackling its passenger station problems, as far as possible retaining, adapting and refurbishing existing buildings where such a course is sensible but getting rid of those structurally unsound, quite unsuitable in size and of little architectural merit. Larbert was a good example of the latter category and its replacement is admirable as are those at Motherwell, both Falkirk stations and a number in the Strathclyde PTE area. To anyone contemplating a study on the ground of Scottish stations the reward will be considerable but the advice must be to do so as soon as possible because, as already suggested, the extension of destaffing and the threats of storm and vandalism could well lead to the loss for ever of some choice buildings.

Above:
Dumfries station was photographed in October 1988 looking towards Glasgow. The buildings are in fine external condition and show many characteristics of Glasgow & South Western station style. The ornate iron lamp standards will be noted, and also the enormous Caledonian goods warehouse in the right background. *J. L. Stevenson*

Below:
At the Great North of Scotland's station at Inverurie in April 1978, only the down side building remained, its once extensive verandah greatly reduced. Normally all traffic uses this platform. Class 27 No 27004 is seen here with the saloon conveying the Board chairman on a tour of the Region. *J. L. Stevenson*

Below right:
A view of Blair Atholl in June 1988 looking towards the start of the 18-mile climb over the Grampians. The goods shed remains beyond the main building and in the left background stands the engine shed which used to provide the banking engines. *J. L. Stevenson*

Photo Feature:

Shadows of Industrial Steam

During 1985, Falmouth Docks restored Hawthorn Leslie No 3597/1926 to working order. It found use as the regular working engine when the Sentinel diesel was being overhauled. On 2 January 1986 it is seen alongside No 4 dock at the end of its day's work. *Graham Hancock*

The 1970s saw the end of most commercially operated industrial steam traction in the United Kingdom. Industrial settings often provided a dramatic backcloth to small working locomotives as they performed their humble duties of moving wagons about. Many worked on connecting lines through short stretches of countryside, and some faced the most steep gradients on atrocious track. All are now a memory.

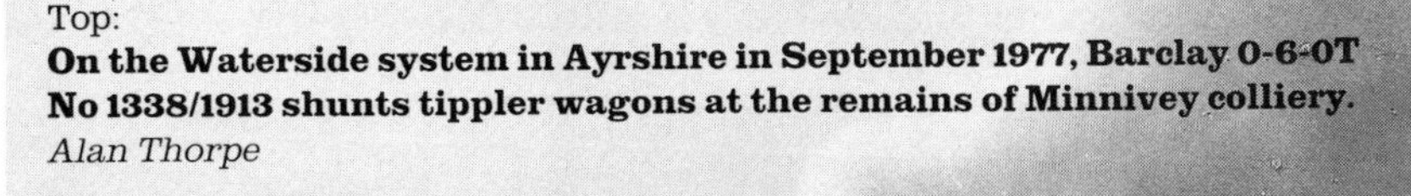

Top:
On the Waterside system in Ayrshire in September 1977, Barclay 0-6-0T No 1338/1913 shunts tippler wagons at the remains of Minnivey colliery.
Alan Thorpe

Top right:
Bedlay colliery shunter No 9 collects empties from the exchange sidings in September 1977, before propelling them back to the colliery sidings. The 0-6-0T was built by Hudswell Clarke (works No 895) in 1909. *Alan Thorpe*

Bottom:
Maerdy's mighty Peckett 0-6-0ST starts empties away from the exchange sidings for Mardy colliery, at the head of the Rhondda Fach, South Wales. *Alan Thorpe*

Above:
Avonside 0-6-0ST *Sir John* lasted into the mid-1970s working on the NCB system centred on Mountain Ash colliery. A beautiful, lined green engine, with a strange homemade chimney, *Sir John* had a wide following among enthusiasts.
Alan Thorpe

Below:
Night falls at Bickershaw colliery on 15 April 1983 as Hunslet 'Austerity' 0-6-0ST No 3776/1952 *No 7* replenishes its water tank outside the engine shed.
Graham Hancock

Grandfather's Railway

Colin Boocock

It was often my pleasure as a teenager at holiday times to travel north from my home at Bournemouth on the 'Pines Express' to Manchester London Road. There I would take a taxi to cross Manchester to Victoria station to board the stopping train to Colne to visit my grandparents. In those days in the 1950s the whole journey was undertaken amid the smoke, dirt and smell of steam locomotives and it occupied the best part of the waking day.

The next two weeks would be filled with trips to the big cities of the north, interspersed with train photography sessions on the fascinating railways local to Colne. It is these local railways about which I write now, looking back with a mixture of pleasure and regret: pleasure through recalling the interest which those railways gave me, and regret that so little remains of them today.

Colne was a small cotton-weaving town at the head of a valley of several such towns in east Lancashire. The railway from Manchester and Preston ran up the valley floor from Accrington through Burnley, Brierfield and Nelson. Colne station was the termination point of several, but not all, of these trains, which had provided a service to these blackened stone towns with their mills and tall chimneys since Lancashire & Yorkshire Railway days.

Immediately north of Colne station the line changed character completely. The route northwards was formerly of the Midland Railway, and was similarly double tracked but otherwise rural in nature. This was the border country between Lancashire and Yorkshire, and the scenery was essentially Yorkshire with lush pastures flanked by dry stone walls, backed by hills crowned with purple moorland. This was the Craven country. The railway served the small town of Earby, from which trailed the short branch to Barnoldswick; onward from Earby the railway meandered a few miles further north before curving east to join the Carlisle-Leeds main line just west of Skipton.

Engine spotters at Colne station, the very few that were to be seen there, were served with quite some variety, though many trains in both directions were dominated by handsome and competent two-cylinder 2-6-4Ts of Stanier and Fairburn types hauling ex-LMS non-corridor stock in rakes of up to eight coaches.

These trains used the up (to Burnley) and down through platforms at Colne, where the copious platform awnings served to keep the frequent rain or drizzle off passengers and enthusiasts alike. Access from one platform to the other was through a shallow, narrow and dark subway which linked with the street level booking hall. The station buildings on the stone-flagged platforms were of smoke-blackened millstone grit. There was a north end down bay platform, normally used for stabling a push-pull train during its layover, though presumably the bay was originally there to provide space for a Skipton connection out of arrivals from the Lancashire & Yorkshire line.

Behind the north end of the up platform was a small goods yard dominated by a huge building still lettered (in the 1950s) 'Lancashire & Yorkshire Railway Goods Warehouse'. This yard was usually shunted by a former L&YR 0-6-0.

If one wanted to see all the stations southwest of Colne on the line to Burnley one had best to catch the push-pull train to Rose Grove. This was a marvellous antiquity known as 'Little Billy' to my grandfather. Two maroon carriages with gated doorways (in later years replaced with modified standard LMS stock) were propelled by a L&YR 2-4-2T based at Rose Grove shed west of Burnley.

The push-pull would leave Colne with the engine pushing from behind, crossing the tall, curved viaduct across the valley. Passing the long, wooden carriage sheds on the left and carriage sidings on the right, the line ran behind the houses towards Nelson. Even in those days there was little discernible green between the towns. The first stop was at the smallest station or halt I had ever seen in Britain, consisting of a few sleepers, a lamp, and a standard LMS board proclaiming this to be Bott Lane halt. The carriages had low steps on which passengers could alight or board the train.

Next stop was the island platform at Nelson itself, well canopied in

Below:
The Lancashire cotton town of Colne sits on its hill overlooking the valley as 'Crab' 2-6-0 No 42825 leaves with a Blackpool excursion on 29 July 1956. The ex-L&YR carriage sheds are on the right, with extra carriage sidings to the left of the line.
Colin Boocock

L&YR style. From here it was a short sprint down the valley to Brierfield, then we called at another halt, Reedley Hallows in the outskirts of Burnley.

Burnley Central was a grim, stone station on a curve, quite well situated for the centre of this town which served as the main commercial and shopping centre of this end of the valley. I remember watching here an ancient, small 0-4-0T with squared saddle tank bringing coal wagons from Burnley colliery into the station yard behind the up platform.

The line now climbed uphill, the 2-4-2T wheezing gently as we passed the rows of steeply roofed terraced houses to call briefly at Burnley Barracks station. Just beyond the town, the double track railway from Todmorden and the Hebden Bridge line, which had its own station at Burnley Manchester Road, trailed in from the left. We were near our journey's end as the push-pull passed the Rose Grove marshalling yard in the hollow on the left, drawing to a halt alongside the island platform.

Just beyond the road overbridge one could gain access to Rose Grove shed (armed with a permit) where L&YR 0-6-0s and 2-4-2Ts were always on display, together with WD 2-8-0s and '3F' 0-6-0Ts, or even the occasional LMS '7F' 0-8-0. In the last year or two of the push-pull service, before Bott Lane and Reedley Hallows disappeared from the railway map, BR Standard 2-6-2Ts of the 84000 series took over these workings and the L&YR 2-4-2s were retired.

On some days I would take a train to Skipton, always hoping for a compound 4-4-0 or a 'Crab' 2-6-0 to break the monotony of the 2-6-4Ts. The first stop out of Colne was at the village of Foulridge (whose attractive station buildings now grace Ingrow on the Keighley & Worth Valley Railway). Then there was a sprint past a canal and more fields before we arrived at Earby. The short Barnoldswick branch was by then closed, but in the early 1950s it boasted its own 'Midland' push-pull train, a Johnson 0-4-4T and two ex-MR non-corridor coaches.

After Earby the Skipton train chuffed its meandering way to the small country stations at Elslack and Thornton-in-Craven before the Leeds-Carlisle main line came into view. We passed the engine shed on our right and came to a stand in one of the south side platforms at Skipton station. These platforms were shared with trains for the Ilkley line via Embsay, trains which could boast a Class 4P compound 4-4-0 or a Fowler 2-6-4T at the head, but would more likely as not have another Stanier 2-6-4T.

A day's train-watching at Skipton would witness a lot of Class 5s on freights, a 'Jubilee' or two, and rebuilt 'Royal Scots' on the 'Thames-Clyde' and 'Waverley' named expresses. '8Fs' and 'Crab' 2-6-0s would appear, and the occasional Ivatt 2-6-0 or compound 4-4-0.

On other days I would cycle from my grandparents' house and take photographs by the lineside in the Colne area: a Class 5 on a Skipton to Blackpool train; a 'Crab' from Newton Heath; a solitary Ivatt 2-6-2T or Fowler 2-6-4T; and the inevitable taper boilered 2-6-4Ts. Once I saw an excursion from somewhere deep in Yorkshire arrive at Colne behind a 'foreign' visitor — a 'B1' 4-6-0. This was exchanged for a LMS engine for the run on to Blackpool, and the 'B1' was turned on Colne's ex-L&YR turntable near the carriage sheds. The Midland turntable at the north end of the station had long since been abandoned.

Soon my holiday would draw to a close and it would be time to go south, to home. I would leave on the star train of Colne's working day — the 8 o'clock to London Euston. A Class 5 4-6-0 would be sitting at the head of five or six Stanier corridor coaches in the up platform. At 8am the engine would hoot and we would move smartly off across the viaduct and down the valley, calling only at the main stations: Nelson, Burnley Central, Rose Grove, Accrington. Here the train would take the Blackburn route (not the more usual

Top:
On the same day, Class 5 4-6-0 No 44692 pulls out of Colne on the Midland section with a train for Skipton. *Colin Boocock*

Above:
Stanier Class 4 2-6-4T No 42546 enters Foulridge station with a Skipton to Colne stopping train on 21 July 1955. The station buildings have since been re-erected by the Worth Valley Railway at its station at Ingrow. *Colin Boocock*

direct line via Ramsbottom to Bury and Clifton Junction) calling at Blackburn and Bolton before the race to Salford and the slow approach to Manchester Victoria. We would then meander round the back of Manchester and Ashton, eventually to reach Stockport in time to be shunted on the back of the 10am (?) from Manchester London Road to Euston. I would either go on this train via London to Bournemouth, or wait at Stockport to join the through southbound 'Pines Express', a slower but more enjoyable run as it reached the south coast by way of Bath Green Park and the Somerset & Dorset line. By then Colne, and Grandfather's railway, seemed a long way away.

Today much has changed. Passengers from Manchester have to go via Blackburn: indeed Colne trains start at Preston and connect at Blackburn into and out of the Manchester Pacers. Accrington no longer has the triangle connection with the Bury line. Rose Grove shed's site is now part of the motorway which runs up the valley to just behind Nelson. Burnley Central station has a modern, simple set of station buildings. At Nelson the track singles. At Colne there is just a single platform and a small passenger shelter — and one buffer stop at the end of the line.

Colne today has no signals, no carriage shed, no sidings, no goods yard, no down bay, no signalboxes, no freight trains, no trains for Skipton (and no Grandfather). Every hour or so a Class 142 diesel two-car set slides across the viaduct and calls at the single platform. The driver changes ends, the guard closes the doors, and the train leaves the way it has just come. Colne then sits quietly on its hill overlooking the valley, with no train sounds until the next Pacer arrives.

There is nothing to hold my attention there now.

Top:
'Little Billy' crosses Colne viaduct. Former Lancashire & Yorkshire Railway 2-4-2T No 50652 propels the 12.15pm push-pull to Rose Grove on 21 July 1955.
Colin Boocock

Above:
Ex-L&YR Barton Wright 0-6-0 No 52319 shunts the small goods yard at Colne in 1953. *Colin Boocock*

Below:
At the north end of Colne station was this classic Midland Railway anti-trespass notice, still extant and fully lettered in July 1956! In the immediate background can be seen the derelict Midland turntable pit. *Colin Boocock*

Below right:
A day's visit to Skipton station would produce many impressive sights. WD 2-8-0 No 90273 takes the Ilkley road with a heavy chemical tank train on 20 April 1957. *Colin Boocock*

Left:
Bott Lane halt, between Colne and Nelson, was a very basic station! L&Y 2-4-2T No 50655 stops briefly there in summer 1954 while working a Colne to Rose Grove push-pull service, to allow passengers to alight using the leading carriage's folding steps. *Colin Boocock*

Below:
Later the same day Fowler 2-6-4T No 42380 leaves the east end of Skipton station with the 4.15pm to Bradford Forster Square via the main line. *Colin Boocock*

Handsome Compound 4-4-0 No 41068 stands at Skipton awaiting departure with the 4.45pm to Bradford via Ilkley. *Colin Boocock*

Spot the difference

Photo -quiz

Part One

Spot the Difference

Can you find the 10 differences between these two photographs?

Where was the original photograph taken?

(Answers on page 79)

Part Two

Photo-quiz

The following six photographs contain scenes which may not be all they seem! Can you answer all six questions?

1. Starlings flock on the 25kV overhead cables outside Glasgow Central station. Why are they not electrocuted?
2. Drinking water for humans and dogs! Where is this unique edifice?
3. Using your skill and judgement, can you say in what country was this photograph taken?
4. The Class 303 electric units were built for the Glasgow suburban network; the Class 33 diesel locomotives are well known as Southern Region locomotives. How come they came together in regular service in this 1983 photograph?
5. What is wrong with this photograph of a 125 power car reflected in a carriage window at Penzance?
6. Mk 2e InterCity coaches — but where was this 1988 photograph taken?

2
1863
FOR YE DOGS

1313

CS39B
33026
4

5

6

Wordsearch

Part Three
Wordsearch

In the matrix below are the names of 17 preserved steam locomotives. See if you can find them. Some letters are used more than once, and six names are in separate words located apart in the square.

S	B	G	D	R	A	L	L	A	M	N
I	L	O	R	D	N	E	L	S	O	N
R	F	L	E	E	U	L	B	R	M	O
L	O	D	E	D	E	F	I	A	N	T
A	S	T	O	W	E	N	U	O	L	L
M	S	S	E	O	F	D	L	T	N	I
I	E	T	P	R	E	O	E	O	P	M
E	H	A	E	R	I	K	Y	L	F	A
L	C	R	T	A	C	F	H	T	O	H
D	U	K	E	O	R	A	D	N	I	L
E	D	N	R	E	N	O	L	A	H	C

When you have found all the names the letters which are left spell the name of an old preserved 0-6-0T in Yorkshire.

The really determined puzzler will also find 23 sets of initials which belong to railways, past or present, at home or overseas. A real teaser this! Can you find them, and write down what they mean?